Love & Death

Love & Death

Greatest Hits

Renée Gregorio

Joan Logghe

Miriam Sagan

TRES CHICAS BOOKS

Cover art :: *Chitipati* (Sanskrit) or *Dutro Dagpo* (Tibetan)
Nepalese Thangka painting, c. 20th century, private collection

Authors photograph :: Anouk Jutta
(*Miriam Sagan, Joan Logghe, Renée Gregorio*)

Book design :: JB Bryan

Set in Sabon

ISBN :: 978-1-893003-03-3

Tres Chicas Books
P.O. Box 417
El Rito, New Mexico 87530

Contents

JOAN LOGGHE

MIRIAM SAGAN

Renée Gregorio

X at the Threshold

1

You fall in love with a stranger
to become someone else,
to take on the body of that voice
as your own. Who is it?
Who is it? The sound could be
a bird's cry. It is so familiar.

Sometimes you can hear a voice's
echo as much as you can the voice.
Go down into the body of that voice,
strange and friendly at once,
let it cover you, unmask you, give you
another shape. Can the original
momentum of desire last?

2

There's part of us that knows
before language. I speak in the tongue
of my ancestors, foreign words,
familiar island of hilltowns, tears
of my grandfather.

I am moving in and out
of a myriad of sensations
that have to do with space and growth,
with the song that is claiming my body.
I see myself running ahead

and myself in other clothes
staying behind.

I go back to the original momentum
of desire. Kissing: a release from self-
definition, self-boundary, entering
the wave of the primitive breath.

It's a matter of shape.
There's more to grow into.
A matter of filling.

3
What's lost is childhood,
that urgency of play.
The voice of that earlier time.
I feel healed by that voice,
rich and round as a ripe peach.
It splits me. The glove of it
circles my hand. In it I believe
in the salvation of making.
The voice as gatekeeper.

Here, I try to be neither
scattered nor torn, but open
to the other voices.
I repeat history
like repeating a prayer
over and over
till its heard or answered.

X: The Space Between

1.

I am a beast who wants her own cage, now and then,
who wants anonymity, another name, no traces.
I wanted to move with him in that dark.
To wear his skin—luminous beast, slippery cave
of words. I can become drugged with words,
afraid of return to my body. But not afraid
of opening. Not afraid of the rose or the lotus
or any particular flower of awakening.
I want to be split open. That is both the problem
and the cure. Split open by another's voice,
the sound of it like wild fire circling me,
elegant circle of burning. Utter consumption.

There are times it is necessary to be
hopelessly in love with what is different
from what we know. How does one carry so much
wanting? I carry it while asking the question.

2.

I dreamt of a man's leg with a scar on it
in the shape of an X. The scar tissue
rose up out of his skin, crossing over of wound
onto wound. What could cut him that way,
I thought. Mysterious shape of old aching.
What battle in him could cause that shape—
the wild and domestic, male and female,

drunk and sober, spontaneous and reflective.
Split by the force of his own desire.

3.
Relationship: fitting two parts together
that being as paradoxical into one working unit
made up of the paradox. Sharing thought
across an intimate space without disappearing.
The truth is both in the drawing-towards,
and in the impossibility of utter merging.
The territory of X.

We speak anyway, our psyches belonging
to the same wide sea. We become enormous waves
of breath and light. Words rise in the dark air
like fish do. If we're lucky, we catch some,
keep them alive, infuse them with our own breath.

Sex does what writing does, sometimes better.
That entering the darkness, rising whole.
The persona, unmasked,
revealing unnamed constellations
already formed in the cosmos,
waiting for you to take their shape on as your life.

The Final X

Leaving felt somewhat like suicide: the intentional
killing-off, stripping away the vestments of home.
Yet also like being born, the coming up
out of the dark into the light, the cry
at the sudden, sharp intake of breath.
If I had nowhere to go I also
had everywhere—the childless woman, bleeding.

Days worn threadbare with searching,
trying to find the sound my own name makes.
I learn to fall over someone
else's arms, crashing onto the mats,
X of bodies, peculiar and singular kind
of release I must have—protecting myself
from myself.

Desire is imagination's best offering.
A man calls at midnight on the full moon.
It's the old story: I want to know what's hidden
and the only way is *through* and *urgent*.
The voice at the far end of the telephone
wire spills. I hold it, hot and dark as my own blood.
Slowly, in the space that is both healing and nightmare,
I remember there's room for all the voices.

Wanting to be stronger and weaker than I am,
the branch in the wind, I spread myself thin
next to the trickle of water in the arroyo,

listen to the sound running down to the river.
I walk into this final settling on the other side
of desire, not expecting someone else
to be my vehicle for transformation. I live
in X's extremes. A stranger becomes
the sudden recipient of my truth—
hidden, numinous water table of grief,
river we swim in that is the same river.

Your bare hand
holding space between us.
I match you finger for finger.

Circling Orgasmic

In this rapid moment
        I have wanted to hear you
                in my mouth

I breathe the subtle
        scent your skin
                gives off

look at erotic drawings in a book
        get turned on by odd positioning
                the geometry of lovemaking
                        think of old equations the various ways
                        1 & 1 have made 2

Your presence was something I passed
        through something I could
                almost name

I can't recall your hands
        pressed against my flesh
                or how your sweaters were too big for me

I can't recall why you came to me
        what we might have exchanged

It's like the hunger of that small
        bird scratching for food
                the snow deep over any possible nourishment

I wanted to kiss you
　　　for a long time
　　　　　become raw with it

I am wildly divided
　　　I want an anonymous sexual encounter
　　　　　in which I am not held responsible
　　　　　　　for anything

I want to enter desire
　　　clearly like diving
　　　　　into cold mountain water

I follow my body
　　　to the places it wants to go
　　　　　enter what's sacred
　　　　　　　take it into me
　　　a communion wafer melting
　　　　　on my tongue
　　　　　　　down into the place words are formed

My desire overtakes me
　　　like prayer

I become articulate
　　　for you, call you comrade, friend

Overnight words rise
　　　like angels

And I wear you
        a new piece of flamboyant
                clothing I am proud of

Our legs wrap around each
        other skin and scars wrapped
                until we sleep
                        breathing each other's air

You are my conversation
        my arc of the circle

The opera music on that jukebox
        reaches its wild hand into me
                pulls the ancestors out of my blood

Sometimes I think I'll never
        find my way home
                in love with possibility as I am

I could go from one man's
        lovemaking to the next
                accept it all into me
                        like taffy at a park
                somewhere in a childhood summer
                        thinking it was my due

I'm in love with an idea
        of unrequited love

nothing to do with any real person
one can't love real people in the same way

I am simply trying to name it—
the destroyer, the dark woman who wants
what she wants when she wants it

I go forth with all my fear
all my courage
all dumbness and intelligence
warmth and aloofness and sensuality
toward the dark abyss of sex

I was happy to circle "orgasmic"
on the form at the doctor's office today

I walked around my house
trying to remember
the border of my own skin

My body opened to you
bottomless
It's the talking that keeps me hot

I felt all boundaries dissolve
our sexes didn't matter
And although we got there
with our bodies, it was our bodies
that felt superfluous in the end

Your eyes became unspeakable water

I'm after a river   a season   a sharpening
        a wetness   a scent   your hands pushing into mine
            a drive   a luminosity   a liquid   a fever
                something I can't bleed away

I hold strong coffee,
the morning soft with longing—
outside, spring snow.

Measuring the Distance

The distance between her lovers' beds
is a wrench, a scythe, a hammer, a rake and hoe.
The distance, a hair's breadth, a wolf's face,
a shimmering robe, a sheet's thickness. The distance
is familiar like the space between the twin beds of brothers.
The sound of rain on adobe or the constant drip
from a tiny leak in the ceiling evoke this distance.
It is a black key caught down a thin hole.

You have to face the underside of everything, lived with
or tasted. There's a terror in giving the self away,
a fish caught at the end of its hook. I remember
the strength of what was then passing swiftly between us,
the rawness at the center, the daring to begin.
In an uprooted world, a slightly shocked fervor
runs in the animal-scented air.

I dream of sleeping in an old apartment that was once mine.
I was afraid to sleep in someone else's place,
even though I had the key. I want memory to be
without aching. I build correspondences.
What will I say to the woods and the stalks of corn?

He didn't want explanations or fever,
didn't want her lips or confessions,
or to remember falling asleep in her bed,
or waking with terror at an open window.

It's embarrassing to be in one place for too long,
but what's too long, and who's noticing?

Intelligent choice is exquisite torture.

Bird-Death

I beat your heart. What never gets said leaks
off the tip of this pen, out the strands in your paintbrush.
What never gets said is the next blotch of red
in a strange woman's crotch, is the next face
with huge aqua-eyes and a spiked tongue.
For me, what doesn't hit the airwaves festers,
explodes here, quiets. I don't want to wake
in a fever of explanations. I want your will
to break my silence. I dream of return to forgotten
things, the river's severe wind to its source,
the rightness in the heart that drew us together.
I refuse silence. Do you know how the river
winds in excruciating twists to its source? The fish
are hunted. Trust is the slow center.
I bury my father's strangeness. I enter
a chamber without sounds. The morning's fever
takes me, then is gone. The question of death
is a bird's thump on the window. The sound
is too soft, too cushioned, its dying swings
like a badly hinged door in the wind.

It's Raining In Augusta

I'm drawn to the harsher seasons,
wind blasting against my chest,
against each grain of wood I clutch.
I want to pare it all down to nothing,
eliminate worn pieces of cloth from my wardrobe,
swim near eroding banks in the old river,
silence the voices that speak in my ears,
invent in silence. But some days I'm caught
in my own skin; there's nowhere to go.
Somewhere, on the other side of the earth,
a man grows old without me, disintegrates.
I dream of him with a severed arm.
Sex was part of everything: the zoo,
the dog's life, the way he splashed words
on an empty page, the shiver from wind,
his heavy yawn. Everything. Now,
I carry the priest's voice at confirmation,
asking *what is pious?* I carry the scent
of incense in the Catholic Church. The black
wrought iron railing crawls on my back,
his hands under my shirt. I wanted anonymity,
to be part of the slur of people
crowding down the stairs at Euston Station.
Instead, I carry the imprint of hotel names,
the remembered desire for my skin,
a fragile green bird with red wings.
I left a scent of French perfume in the white rooms.
I left silence, so they could listen to themselves.
I left pulsing veins, a leaf with its own boundary.

Letter to the Heart of My Far Country

You're like them, with your strangling hands,
your smoky breath. You're like the prisoners
you teach, your hands killing, refusing
to move pen across page, address an envelope,
my name emblazoned on its front.
You strangle what you once loved,
the corpse stretched out in front of you.
You trip on my corpse, don't you?
But I'm not dead.

I read your poetry for messages from you.
I read, *No, don't you ever come see me.*
I can hear your voice whispering hoarsely in my ear.

The dark surrounds us. I don't know where we are.
Energy changes hands. Can we meet where no one can see?
I want something tangible from you; even a stone
with a hole in it would do. I want to ask:
Is forgetfulness necessary for survival?

I'm not convinced. I'm crazy with your voice in my blood.
It's dug out of the earth like that sculpture in Thoreau;
the carved holes invite me in. I crawl into one's dark shape.
You're next to me in another hole.
We burrow and scrape; the walls won't give way.
I scratch the surface of what contains you.

I know the numbered buses of your city, their routes
and timetables. I think of the roads you travel, wonder
where you go. Is it anywhere? Or just further
into your own grief, the grief you name a prisoner's?
I live on the side of a mountain. I am rooted in this earth.
You didn't let me say goodbye.

I imagine slipping away from you,
saying one final line, watching curtains fall.
I walk off stage, the rigid grip of last words
in my jaw. I release the memory of you from the center
of what I've become, change costumes, walk down that city street
unrecognizable, without my former name, without speech.

What was open closed suddenly, a door in a windstorm.
I didn't know it was coming.
For months, I looked for you on the mesa; I wanted you back.
I'd stretch out on the earth and stare at the sky.
Its largeness was all that could hold me. Its endlessness.
I would've died in that city.

Now, I'll look for you in the open, not to resurrect you,
but to make sure you exist. I doubt our exchange.
I would like to sit across a table from you and talk,
see the new lines in your face,
the sour way you could look. I would like to hear
your accent when you say *love*,
reach across the empty space,
connect my hand with yours, dare to look you in the eyes,

not have you turn away. Yes,
I'm out on the desert walking,
and I'm headed in your solitary direction.
I must know who you are without me.

Partings

In the end, they cannot make the crossing.
They're left on the harbor's edge,
waiting without schedules, without a weather report,
for a ship that would contain them.

His baggage weighed in too heavy, hers
not enough. The authorities denied them
passage, weighing all possibilities,
each coming up: *No, we do not have the space you desire.*

She is weeping, she is weeping, and the soft shields
of her eyes are falling; she cannot see distances.
He is weeping, he is weeping under the glass
of his eyes, tinted to hide his profusion of tears.

They turn to each other. When once they would have
embraced, they can now only nod, reach out
a hand, feel the bones on the other's face,
turn again toward the wave's sudden swell.

Loose Change

How to manage this correspondence,
or any, for that matter.
Leaving without sign or signature,
a hand pushed into concrete before it dries.
Yet another set of unlived possibilities,
a sudden hailstorm just as suddenly over.
Imprints, sketches on the underside of skin,
words etched into new places, refusing
to accept the impossibility of anything.
There's nothing but sagebrush here,
what was once ocean turning forever
into its absence, but the air still breathes salt.
Nothing much lasts, not even this absence
in its present form. But some decisions
are definite, knife-slicing, full of blood.
and in all that red, all the daring to refuse.
Perhaps nothing lasts. But there's still
seventy-two cents worth of loose change
on the carpet, and few feathers
from a dead, red-breasted bird
the cat dragged in before they made love.

Valentine

It's the breath I want from you
night after night in whatever bed
we find   the breath   that comes
and goes from your mouth into
my ear   my hair   as if
all night you're telling me a story
without end   and I am taking in
what makes you live, what's
killing you. It's your breath
I can't live without, your breathing
that makes its way into me
those moments like crystals
you said   and crystals are real.
It's the passion I'm after
the opening to our breathing together
the sound of your breath
reverberating through my head
your hands grabbing me in the dark
as if to say: *no you don't have to go*
the memory of your lips on my hair
your fingers running through each
strand of black.

Rushes

Mostly, I want to go to sleep
realizing there is love in my life,
and then I want to stop dreaming
of houses I don't live in except in dreams—
perfect and singular, with more rooms
than I'd ever need.
I want to throw away my old things,
start again from nothing, rearrange
my cells in the shape of birds of paradise,
or blue irises or the sound of blues or the taste
of olive oil on anchovies or I want to feel
like a mirror does or a black hole
or the long shimmering journey of a falling star.

I really only want to be something other than I am.
Doesn't everybody? The blues. If she'd take me back.
If he'd take me back. If we never let go. Walk away.
Just walk away. Everyone tries to until one day, one night,
you simply can't and staying is all there is, bodies fusing
under the wide night sky. Obliterate the blues?
Impossible.

The night is as restless as we'll let it be.
You can run the streets and bars looking
for love or something like it, or not.
The madness of living with all that is possible,
afraid of disappearing without boundary.

But there are seconds when the gods meet in the air
between two faces, when all is believed in.
This morning's sunlight pulsates
in the cleft of the aloe leaves.

Trying on the skins of possible lives,
years came together, years went away.
One learns to live in the immediate jungle,
planting gardens at every turn, letting
the grass grow unwieldy. There isn't as much time
as you think, isn't much time at all.
Kissing at dusk in an unknown doorway.
Kissing anywhere. His hand rests
on the black silk of her leg; as he lifts it away,
his handprint etched into the silk.

Closets within closets. The earth under rocks.
Shadows. What resides there? What goes on
in a darkened room when no one's in it
and all the doors are locked?

Concentrating on the shift in every cell.
Thinking of falcons, how they hover in perfect stillness
above their prey, how startling to watch their waiting,
simply waiting. The absolute patience of their maneuvering.
Their inner timing. The corners of his eyes.
That gnawing at the edges. Heat rising from groin.
I keep seeing the falcons. The wildness of edges.
Straining towards the light like the wandering Jew
in the dark corner of my kitchen.

The memory of the New York skyline across the Hudson.
I'd look at the skyline and think of you,
how you were always just out of reach, always perfect
and defined and distant as those high rises, reaching
across water I couldn't travel. How incredible it is to make love
to a man who doesn't mind blood. In the next breath,
the knowledge that nothing is about endings.
At times there's nothing beyond skin touching, tongues
finding each other. Let's hear it for the scent of strangeness,
the forbidden, the difficult, the rich, the strong,
the largeness of his body, an accent unlike my own.

Once, I thought I would stay in the north of England,
some border town on an island, living with a man
who all his life carried the name of another man.
But I couldn't bear the thought's weight, never sure
of the words that sprang green and full of hope
from his British lips. Caught in the word's absolute bareness,
he lived, over and over, in the stories he created of himself.
I had to go from him. He had difficulty recognizing himself
in a mirror. The banshee's keening reached across
the border from Scotland, her wail without shape,
haunting the landscape. I wanted him to touch
the blood on the prison wall's graffiti, to feel the demons
residing there. I woke to the same startling window,
opening to tears. Which one lasts through the other's
changing? Gone, as they all are, into the silence,
a part of the air we breathe.

Silent Dialogue

You want to be free of so many things,
yourself for one. And the heavy vigas.
You want to be free of the driving wind,
the empty canvas, the wilting strawberry plants.

I don't know how to walk here, among the ruins.
I trip on the rough-edged stones. It's too dry;
I want to water everything without asking.
The wind blows hard, delivering a whisper of *father*.

A silent, invisible yoke. You dream of morphine.
Another addiction, directing you to another sort of death.
But you say in the dream, *I have you and I don't want to die.*
Light against stone. The silence of a clenched muscle.

Some days I think I want to get married.
It's a matter of linguistics; I want to say *husband*.
By the Rio Chiquito, Catanya told me lobsters mate for life.
I thought of how many halves of couples I'd eaten.

I'm sorry; I was hungry. When we woke this morning,
we spoke without words of the wide, green field in the distance.
It was before the alarm went off, after the shrill of coyote.
Quick lightning split Pedernal.

It was more than the curve of your bent elbow, more
than the words we said that kept us together, more

than that particular intersection. We saw the fragile
leaf of the unflowering pansy and felt afraid.

A song is building inside the lining of our throats.

waking slowly
I place my hand on his face
all around us, air
turns from fall to winter:
our breath begins to leave a trace.

Two

It's been two weeks and two days
since you died.
The morning before: two *I love yous*
breathless over telephone wires
and then you were already mostly gone.
I think of you when I watch things airborne,
mostly birds that suddenly fly right in front
of my car, like never before. Two nights ago
in Glorieta I watched all the stars rise, one by one,
and picked the brightest to be you. Today, Steve told me
he saw the swell of your liver in x-ray and I knew
you had to die. He said he had to help you into bed
that last night, all the weight of you measured in his small hands,
and that made me remember the time I left you
drunk on the brick floor of my house because I couldn't
move you even one inch—I tried—cowboy boots and wide-brimmed
hat and all, and how the next day you gave up drinking
and I moved in with you and your hands
pulled me in all night long and later you'd call and call, pulling
the laughter out of me, complaining about all those fish
you could never catch. But, dear one, with me the line reached
all the way to the back of the throat, didn't it? We found the words
and the breath for some pure strand of connection that never ended,
even now, though it's so difficult, I talk to you in my car,
on the tennis court, as I sleep and as I wake the full body
of you haunts me and it's you
I went the farthest with and the longest, with you I learned
the possibility of endurance, the necessity of stopping and gazing,

the marathon of bad art and what it is to keep making
and making and making—against every strain of disbelief,
against the cold and crushing winters and the dryness and the weeds
and the crumbs between the cracks in the floor and the mud-splattered
windows that no one could clean but you. I planted lots of seeds
in our yard. They have grown to flowers now that come back,
year after year, more abundant with time. You planted two aspen trees
in the front yard that we watered together. They're growing, Bill.
Every last seed has sprouted, takes root, reaches up into
what has become your sky.

The Artist's Near-Wife: A Letter

While my hair was still curled with the wet of the East,
I rode my Raleigh hard down the Paseo.
You came by in your Scout, noticing shape,
And we went on living in the village of Lama,
Two large people, without much money or water.

Year one you told me you'd never marry.
I never flinched, being salty.
Raising my head, I looked into your eyes,
Called to by others, I said *No, I am here*.

By year six, no turning back.
I desired my dust to be mingled with yours.
I wanted this union to bring us a child.
You said no. I climbed the lookout.

Year seven, I departed.
I went clear through the canyon, passed by the river of swirling eddies.
I was gone over two years.
Coyote howled in your nights, traffic in mine.

We each went out, forcing the split.
Now I have no home and at yours the grasses are overgrown—
Too deep to clear them away!
The rains come early this summer, the winds.
Your death comes too soon, before you said it all, with lightning
Breaking my sky and your voice no longer.
This hurts me. I grow older.

If you are flying overhead someday through unknown currents,
Please let me know in my dreaming,
And I will come out to meet you
As far as the reddest river.

so disappointed
this early morning—the promised
snowfall already turning
to ice on the pine bough
as my heart clings to old love

This Harsh Desire for Other

He draws me in like the mountains
seem to draw the rain down, furtive
pulling, the way hunger moves
grumbling in the early stages,
asking all,
open-mouthed, anxious.

I've driven down roads with no streetlights,
adrift in huge fields, the horizon unseen
or unreachable. I've felt hunted, running fast,
always something tight to my back.
I'm not afraid anymore.
I want to shake at the root.

I do not say *I love you* on abandoned benches
in deserted parks. I say it on the subway,
noise and people crowding our bodies, the more
inapt the place, the better. I will say it
everywhere. I don't need him here. I conjure him
sharp as the nettle's quick, reverberating sting.

I am at home in silence,
though it can consume like waves
in the Atlantic, so vast
they obliterate breath. I live in awe
of that which is split when once it was whole,
like the Rio Grande gorge divides
the earth's plates into uncrossable chasm.

I have been the stone in the river
a man stepped on to get across.

I've followed the arc of desire far out
into a wild universe. I came to men's voices
with the heart of a little girl.
Does monogamy mean I will never be touched
by another man under the moon's rising light?
I stare at a photograph where a thousand birds
take flight in the space above a woman's head.

I touch his arms, his chest,
I press my hands into flesh
to make him mine, take him into me,
to let all the others drop away.
We broadcast years of information
in a single breath, the air wiser for it.
I didn't know I loved the sound
of two rivers coming together,
or entering someone else's sadness
like a drumbeat, feeling it in the center
of the heart, the hungry self
salivating, this harsh desire for other.

Triangle of Light

There is not much time.
I must tell you everything right away.
How this morning, blurry and tired, I reached
under the kitchen chair to pick up what looked like
something, yet it was simply a triangular patch of light
formed by sun and obstruction.

I come to these words
out of a floating world that's supposed to be made
only of pleasure. I am good at the momentary,
crawling into that triangle of light,
washed out by its intensity.
I hardly know you, yet last night,
driving to Albuquerque alone, my body
craved you, opened to you,
pomegranate spilling sweet seed.

That red stains all of my fingers.
It's you I want to put those fingers in,
wherever you'll let me. You are cruel
to make me burn this way, cruel as March
winds sticking it out through April,
how these nights freeze the daffodils
and the buds on the apricot tree,
how they may never recover to bear fruit.

God Went Away for the Winter, She Said

It's hard between two people.
Some days we walk the clouds of these mountains.
Others I hear only complaints, the straight
lines of will. Embracing the ordinary
is wrestling the winter-god. Note the shifting
color of your skin. What is the same
can gather strength, a rolling snowball,
can be ally, mistress, lover.
Yesterday I woke to three rainbows
on the living room floor, your chest
rising and falling under my splayed fingers.
Today you said *Look at that,* pointing
to the intricate spaces between the piled wood.
It's an accident, you said, meaning the beauty
that arrived outside our window, or
that you noticed it. I have a bar of soap
from Mexico with a man and woman kissing.
My friend's gift. *This brings the man you want
to you,* she said. On the wall there's a photo
of you and me kissing, years ago now, on a patio
in Santa Fe. That alchemy once came to us, will again.
It's hard between two people. In December I wrote:
*Dearest love. This is the world we've always wanted,
our breath rising and falling like one hundred magpies
under the dying lilac bush. The sun is hiding.
We are our own best kindling.*

Bloom

I have had things my way and liked it:
the day split by paper and skin,
orange poppies you pointed at
out the kitchen window cranked open
to air and the sound of chainsaw.
We let the light in.

I like the way you wash me
softly with warm water after
we make love hard, you
all the way to the end of me.
Your eyes let the light in.

Your heart is pounding,
but not with love. I would call it love
but I can hear you say *oh no*
all the way back to a childhood
and a past I know little about.

I ask you what it is you want
from me and you answer: *everything*.
So do I. Especially you backing into me
on the bed, curling into my chest, letting me
kiss your hair and hold you as if you
belonged there. It is like coming home.

I make so much of this
because there is so much to be made.

Today the light between us glares.
I bask in it like any good day of sun,
come away marked with a dark tan.
It is the way you grab my hand,

Hold it away from you,
as much as anything else that makes me
want you. It is also the way you are not
afraid to touch me through to what's behind
the muscle, what's underneath
the blood. You cure me of an old injury
with hands sharp as lightning, soft as turned earth.

You give yourself away wherever you can.
I would gather you up like a precious bouquet,
take your scent in, feed the flowers
cut from their roots till they opened,
petal by petal, in this harsher light of day.

The Long Hill of Garrapata

1.

I always had to climb the long hill of Garrapata to get back to you,
knew the way my aging car would slow for its incline,
knew what the house would smell like when I arrived, its mixture
of wood-smoke and eucalyptus leaf browning on top of the Ashley
and your skin with its paint and sweat and your grey hair caught
under the rim of your Stetson. You'd tell me: I heard you coming
from the bottom of the mountain. We would laugh, knowing
how much we each listened for the sound of the other.
You placed the striped rock from the mesa on a post outside
the front door, named it my homing rock. It worked.

2.

Many years ago, my grandmother called me precious.
I might have been five, looking up at her through clasped
hands, wondering what the word meant. Now I know
the innocence that can only exist before there's a word for it,
that I trusted her utterly to take me down the street to the square
and back home again safely, that there was such a thing as safety
and that I owned it. Death changes all that. Before the word
for death, just the sense of looking out on an empty,
surging sea. The sound of death makes me want
someone's hand to hold, someone who can take me safely home.

3.

Here I am, on the face of the earth without you.
If I dig in the vacant lot that is my garden, I think of your body,
now turned to ashes, feeding the earth that was once our home.

If the wind is strong, I imagine you going places,
just as you used to dance with your feet planted and your arms
swirling like propellers—the violent weather becomes you.
When the hummingbirds feed outside my bedroom window,
you must want to tell me something crucial, so I listen.
I have planted you a thousand times over since your death,
as if through digging, another one like you might find a way into me.

4.
I map this sudden territory of dark the dead occupy,
the other side we know little about, yet now I want to know
what happens in death because you are there and I want to know you,
as I always have. Williams said: *Death/is not the end of it.*
I believe him as I used to believe you when you told me
you loved me, when you said you couldn't go on.

5.
It is quieter here now. On the phone wire,
it is never your voice. We are all growing older
without you. Your death made your daughters
more beautiful. I am watching them, thinking of you.
They carry your weight, made of both thunder and water.
I call them precious. The homing rock takes me to the barrio.
You are my angel. I hear you coming from the back
side of the mountain. There are times you are so noisy
I know death is not where you end.

Reincarnate

we could be trees grown next to each other
only I'd have to be quiet sometimes, you said,
and I said you'd be one of those trees that never stop
swaying, and we could be the harsh resonant beat of drum,
skin stretched taut and the stick   we could be
Coho salmon in Eagle Nest Lake fished for
through 20-inch-thick ice   we could be the lake itself
we could be the smoke in the air between us
in the Ford pickup   we could be the way the road winds
we could be etched fish and bird in stone
we could be the parallel lines
on the highway   we could be the singing bowl
and the wood that elicits its sound   we could be hungry,
on the streets, our palms up   we could be snakes
in desert grass, the dust from stars, the tail of a comet,
the mouse under the bed, the road on a map,
just hands, just mouths, just eyes   we could be
manatees, crows, swallowtail butterflies, the new moon,
or blood and bones again, searching
the root of the other
we could be.

You, my husband, are
the reason I can look straight
into other men's eyes.

The Painted and the Real

The datura in his painting
is not the datura with its sweet,
rich scent hovering over the kitchen table,
though they might look alike
in exacting ways, the white flute
of the two flowers plays different music.

His name is the same as so many men—
uncle, mother's high school sweetheart, ex-lovers.
And yet when I say his name it is new every time,
this air breathing life into its syllables,
ripening the fruit of what's common.

I remember the cherries on the tree in Jacona.
My landlady cried when I left that house,
the ditch running right through the yard,
walks in the *barrancas* made of dust,
sudden paths emerging as my feet planted slowly.

At Hotevilla waiting for the butterfly dance to begin,
we wandered dirt roads soft with longing, sweet with rain.
In the empty-chaired plaza, clearing and preparation,
Hopis passing by as we sat separately watchful.
A butterfly, golden in the early morning light,
appeared over my head, hovered there too briefly to tell.
Later that morning the dancers wore tablitas painted with butterflies.
The real evoked the dance.
Or did the dance evoke what's real?

Already he speaks: *I love you* and I ask
how do you know? I am not rebuking him,
only curious for the ways in which these words
are said or not said, for the difference they make.
I love you opens me as the crooked sting of lightning
opened the sky in Los Alamos this week,
after the rain that blinded us.

Believe me, I want to see everything.
I want, once again, to ask for everything.
This means lovemaking on the grass
behind adobe wall in rain,
later hearing impatience in his voice
over phone wire, then faith that this larger canvas
will find its place on these walls.

Today he said he wants to be the only one.
My heart is a letter bomb: all it'll take is the ripping
open of the envelope to set it off.
It follows the Rio Grande
from Lama to the south valley of Albuquerque,
rich with death and singing, like the earth in this yard,
and how digging down into it, I come quickly to water.

The Storm That Tames Us

We must do more than look
at the flowers. The gardener's pleasure:
labor and the fruits of labor. The digging
and the careful placing of seeds, the tending, the waiting.
When the green shoot first breaks ground,
it is the sound of birthing we like most.

We must begin. We've loved over continents and cultures
to bring ourselves here, on the road between barrio and village,
loving with a yearning toward intelligence,
if intelligence is a kind of fire of the mind.

I have watched you come at me
like watching clouds gather on the far horizon
toward storm. I have watched the storm of you
gather and have felt it in my breasts
like the wet scent of near-rain in the northeast
air of my beginnings, or like smelling sage after rain.

Once, I was in the sky all the way to you, asking:
Is this the territory of my dead?
—endless azure and cotton, the roads
snaking far below. There were lights sparkling
across the distant backdrop of a sprawling city.
I come closer to the buildings that house those lights,
just to see the structure there.

Yes, I'm terrified to begin again, as if beginning
holds already the tenuous seeds of loss, made to break us.
Yet the deads' shadows have circled and embraced us.
I ask myself: What was all that's gone before?
Your hands resonate years of lived desire.
I hear the way the leaves are falling.
I have said yes to the question of union.
I've watched you crawl under the colors
of your death-blanket and didn't turn away.
On Xmas, we came through the church door
at Taos Pueblo, from inner dark to the night's dark,
stunning with fire.

I stood in the courtyard looking under the wooden lintel,
through the doorway into more dark, into the white canopy
held over the queen's head, into the wind lifting
the canopy and, beyond, the smoked sky and air
shot the color of pomegranate. The open door,
and again, the white canopy lifting.

We walk the earth with something like intent
circling our days, leave with something more than intent
taking us away. Do we know the seeds of our dying?
You are the vehicle of my return
to this place of silence where objects begin
to live again. Where your eyes save me.

Last summer, at someone else's wedding, I rose up
out of the crowd of single women, as if lifting an arm
to light a torch I could barely reach. I grabbed

that bouquet out of thin mountain air, out of the grips
of another woman, knowing in my blood I am next.
It was a move of pure instinct, born of waiting.

Labor and the fruits of labor.
Days all you get is the digging.
Days all you get is the fruit.
This storm has arrived to tame us. All these years
the air heavy with it and we knew nothing else.
Now we get the release. At last we get the release.

The Beginning Island

Surrender and celebration in equal measure, we married at Tanah
Barak to the sound of water falling and Sanskrit on the Hindu
priest's lips, faces smiling at us in two languages.

This island, both vast and enclosed, where the scent of nasturtium
rose from the edges of rice fields into our bed. Out the window,
the half-hidden volcano, a fragment of plenty, like what remains of
Sappho.

The second ceremony, in Gloucester on the Atlantic, pulled by
family history and seaweed back to childhood when things happened
easily. We married in Olson's town, bordered by seaweed and rocks
in a circle filled with morning light, showing only the way in.

In the round, green spotted rock wet with sea, I felt the sea's breath,
its waves and light, the surf's pounding in the palm of my hand,
in my skin and heart, like a prayer or a song, the rock's hardness
growing in me like someone else's life, mixed with the ancient sweet-
ness of Italian honey, my father-in-law and grandmother dancing.

A friend writes: *marriage is moving to another country, a different
way of being, another language, another basis of meaning.*

I dismantled the singleness of my life, the solitude as I'd known it,
breaking up and redefining what I'd named as my own.

Out of sheer repetition of vows and ceremony, we married—ritual arithmetic of knowing each other, the ways we are written together now.

Fragile Quartet

1

I have wanted to go toward what I was afraid of—

deep ravine in the thick heat of Bali
gut wrenching crossing,
fear beginning at center, then spreading

like one drop of blackberry
on the white porcelain sink
like blood in the fibers of a shirt

Then I remembered the fragility in the bones of my mother.

2

This making and breaking of words
this making of a home
I can fully inhabit

Unearthing boxes unopened for ten years,
so much flowing out,
and with those pieces of paper, pieces of heart.

3

Over the Sandias, clouds as towers
of moisture and light. I have flown
through thunderheads to meet my husband
down here on an earth clarified by rain,
a grace that washes out what's past

Words emerge at a deep level of form,
invisible and trustworthy as old love letters
in boxes: Can we live with who we've been?

4
Passion determines shape.
In marriage we mix objects
as much as ideas, our house built
from the heart outward, toward habitat

Planes can drop thousands of feet in a second—
how brief our time on earth,

how easily our bones break,
how hard to find wings and hearth
in our two breaths.

Indian Love Song

And did I go to the ends of the earth with you?
    —I did.

And did we ride north on highway 47 to the Palace of
Padmanabhapuram and touch the carved breasts of the gatekeepers
outside Saraswati's chamber?
    —Oh, yes.

And did we ride on nine trains, sometimes clear through the
night, and did we learn from strangers that we'd met them before
somewhere along a road, a river, a path, another journey in another
lifetime, perhaps?
    —It is written, yes.

And did we stand in the halls of worship for the Jains, the Hindus,
the Muslims, the Catholics, and did you dip your fingers in the
clam shell filled with holy water and did I press my ear against the
musical pillar made of granite and touch its liquid song?
    —Together, all of this.

And did the boy on the crowded bus slide his body over to make
room for yours as the elder, not mine as the woman?
    —Yes, and we laughed.

And did we eat idlis, dosas, sambar and coconut chutney till we
didn't want them anymore?
    —Yes, but now it's hard to believe we were once sated.

And did we watch men and women pulling tiny silver fish off the nets and into buckets for selling while the snakes writhed on the sand nearby, trying to find their way back to water?

    —We were afraid of swimming.

And did the priest turn the mirror toward our faces so we could see the god within? And did we see it? And are we whole?

    —We were bathed with seeing.

And did we understand there's no good or bad, big or small, only what is?

    —Sometimes we did.

And could we answer the temple guard's question——"For what purpose do you come here?"—put to us aggressively then, with calm now?

    —Perhaps our presence would hold the answer.

And did we eat enough prawns biryani, fish curry, Keralan parotta and fig and honey ice cream?

    —Never.

And did we occupy different skins in the sea air? Did we make love like the ice cream, like the giant prawns—familiar in concept, but not in magnitude and sweetness?

    —Yes, we met each other as travelers first, husband and wife second.

And did the early monsoon rains clarify us?

    —Of course, we were washed clean.

And did we stand mesmerized by the mustard yellow house near
the town's deep and ancient well, taking in the sound of a man
practicing violin in the front room, the one most open to the street,
how solitary and public he was, did we take this in?
      —It made us want to change the world.

And were we happy where things are never straightforward?
And did we go far into nothing to know everything?
And did our bodies become eyes?

The Question of Death

At 55, what do I long for?—not exactly
the checkout man at Albertson's
who gives me my first senior discount
& I try to dispute it, ask:
"How old does one have to be?"
He answers: "55."
He didn't even ask for identification,
simply knew I'd crossed that threshold.

But this crossing-over, where does it lead?
Do I write a poem about death,
or do I sit down at last
and write my will?
If I practice
a certain fullness of the mind,
where does that take my body?
If I offer myself
and no one comes,
how would I stand for refusal?
In death, is there at last
a quieting of the questions?

Today, I've been married 14 years.
I used to think this a kind of dying,
feared sameness and dailiness, the dependable.
Now I use a wooden stick
to help me down the mountain,
reach for another's hand when crossing

a rough stream, no longer get feisty
when he calls me his wife.
Day after day, a different sunset.

I don't know how to write about my own death,
hear the Hindu man in the train compartment
saying "It is written," although he was talking about
our meeting and parting and meeting again.
Yeah, it is written, this coming and going, this returning.

Maybe I'll come back as a desert apache plume,
a clump of seagrass in the dunes of Provincetown,
the fog that envelopes and releases the hills of Big Sur,
a river that slowly cuts its way through rock,
or a human who has certainty rather than questions.

I'm too busy being born to die,
and anyway death will come.
It will be quiet and rigorous
and ask something of me I had not
thought to ask myself.

Joan Logghe

A Lunch Date with Beauty

I had a lunch date with Beauty.
I was on time
But Beauty was already waiting.

I ordered a dry French white.
We discussed music.
I wanted to put on white gloves
But my thoughts were on bed and food.

We ate silently, intent on flavor.
We were both shy.
We'd been estranged.

I kept glancing at Beauty.
The light was flawless,
The food, delicate.

Skipping dessert
We went to a gallery
Of black and white photography.
I liked the rows of Japanese shoes
Outside the monastery.

I wanted a lens so clean
It could capture the purity
A marriage needs.

I wanted a sea shell purse.
The silver one, the cockle shell.

I wanted a print of Origami birds.
Inside me, the empty place.

It began to drizzle.
We stood by a goldfish pond.
The fish swam like watercolor.

I was there, but partly in Boston.
I was there, but it seemed like San Francisco.
There I stood, but it was too much like Chicago.

I had a lunch date with Beauty.
I paid for Beauty with all I had.
I would take risks daily, pay anything
For an hour with beauty.

Mixed Marriage

My husband with no band, with a barbwire
Voice and a closet full of verbs. My husband
Of lapis lazuli. I gave my husband a power mower
For a wedding. Wed him under a *chuppa*
Of evangelical hammers. I married him, a geisha
To a wok to a blue martin to a box of cornflakes.

I went to the church on a streetcar filled
With carnations. We ate carnations in public, man
And wildfire, husband and furnace. We tried to say
I do, but said, I dare. The minister was hanging
A Japanese scroll in fifteenth century Rivers.
He said, "Do you take the worst and make soup?
Do you take the best and escalate?" We said,
"I sweat," said, "Nobody mention death."

My husband with his Farmer's Almanac heart and
The will of a hundred horsepower lunar calendar.
When we travel life is reduced to nouns: key, clock,
Money. Roadmap, shower. When we marry we take the verb.
Cohabit, fight, apologize. Procreate, launder.
Out of the cast iron nuptials into the consummate fire.

Reading in Bed

Summer closes like a pink snapdragon.
On my birthday with new coral earrings
we lie across the mattress
each turning
our own pages.

Amazonian jungle in your hands
and my Japanese novella,
implicit as a plate of raw fish.
I stroke you as I read
turn and sleep.

I wake in a tea ceremony,
a vessel you handle with decorum.
Water and whisk, there is history,
the scent of green tea
and not a word.

A page turns once.
on the corner of the bed.
In folds, in a heap,
I am that floral orange kimono.

After Making Love

After many days the rains fell
and after angers. The tears-of-feeling rain,
a heat-me-up, moose-in-rut,
left-handed-lover-in-diamond-ring rain.

You melted out of the dinnertime.
Changed into soft shoes, full beard,
traded in your currency for coin. I'm a new car.
You cruised me.

Rented an enormous lover's heart.
Remodeled it for leisure, a Japanese love motel.
All the peninsulas were there
and all the folded ladies.

The Peacemaker was playing
a violin of horse and cat and wood
and I was on the edge of my seat
waiting for the bridge of peace.

The Golden Gate across a lost Brazilian river
painted orange for life. All the species came, the
trees, the beasts of burden, and the lamb.
Deep salmon was served up on a black plate.

In ordinary air you tuned me.
Divine breath breathed me.
Your left leg trailed off the bed.
I wrote and wrote sacred music.

I wrote you down ecstatic
and in our bed perfect. I wrote you
a testimonial speech for the banquet
and gave you seven gold watches

all with my hands.
I put you in time again
out of the delirious
into the lyric.

After Reading Love Lyrics from India

Loving summer night.
The gnats bite, the
insinuations of mosquitoes.
Box elder bugs striped, black
yellow and black on the wall.
We peel off the heat
in layers. We have to talk.
Strip down, insignificant
as bug nonsense.
Later, we get down to business
and turn the light sheets of summer
into tents, where a dark Hindu
woman lies down on top
of the blue god.

A Walk in Talpa in Springtime

Walking past sparrow, giddy, past apple blossom
and cherry bloom on the end of stem.

Through whir of hummingbird.
Walking past fat gray horses lying down

and a man with black suspenders
forking alfalfa.

Iris and lilacs, the ditches run full.
I feel desire, a river there, a pressure.

How many women have walked this road aflame
thinking of lover or husband or God?

Heat of day evaporates the dew
that collects on the lips of spent tulips.

Glorious disease. I ask the Virgin of Guadalupe
to wrap her light around me, as a girdle, to cool me.

Who am I fooling? Today
the robe of Aphrodite is my true garment.

Projection

That man could lead me
To a town where churches ring bells
Matins and vespers.
He leads me to a room
Sun washed and clean
Desks lined with paper,
Velum, watermarked.

That man takes me upstairs to a bed
Made up in pressed white sheets.
He relaxes me. He massages my neck.
He asks me where joy lies for me
And joins me to myself
In the first daylight.

I ask that man if I will see him again.
The clouds in the east flush and change color.
He says, "Your clean room is your art.
Your passion, another sort,
An opening.

Come back to this town when you can.
The bells will ring, the lilacs
Permanently fresh. Come back
To this place each morning
And write me alive."

Won Ton

You said, flashing your Persian eyes,
You wanna eat wanton soup?
But the bowl was chilly and I wanted hot.
With you in the room I couldn't tell.
Every Thursday I'd like to take a man
out for Chinese food, down Cerrillos Road.
And afterward the Western Scene Motel
with fake hacienda rooms.
Imagine my hair grown magically long.
But it's all too Chinese and actual.
I'm married and forty is an itchy time.
Forty is for fortune cookies.
I like his lips, his voice and his hair.
His mind I'm not crazy about, but
He is young, a western scene,
a fortune on a white slip.

Pavilion

The jazz band played
on a pavilion. Couples danced
close to the unlit edge.
I was admiring the piano player's shoes
black and shiny. You walked in
right out of the Sixties and I said,
not missing a beat, "Hi Lover."

You once said when we're forty-five
we'll meet, compare divorces.
You never married, I did,
up to the chin in family.
I can still laugh at how I loved you
when we were twenty.
We didn't ride that elevator
up and back a hundred times,
we just dreamed around the edges
of the dark.

I kept everything I ever got from you,
poems from the Japanese, notes
hidden in textbooks.
I kept how it was I loved you.
It's that kind of love I've read in books,
a Russian novel, an old country.
A man and woman aging far apart,
trains run between them daily
but they never ride.

The Homeless

All night, since I can't escape into your bed
and play in the adult leagues
where the man with perfect pitch
and the most foolish woman of the twentieth century
reunite and copulate a population of lovers,

That dark militia with their uniform of hands
reach into my sleep and beg hours,
with their unwashed fingers, undress me.
They say, "A hot meal. Spare change."
They say, "Please tuck me in."

Every block has life embarrassing itself.
Asleep on the streets on cardboard,
the army of our poor. A part inside
can't hide anymore, climbs out to beg
with paper cups from what is rich.

Just because we don't make love
it doesn't go away. Your hands
weighted on top of the table.
I say, with my fingers, "A hot meal."
Washed in all my parts, "Please tuck me in."

I leave town tomorrow.
Again, on Thursday night, the homeless,
awake with their eyes no one
will meet, stares that evaporate
stars.

This new Calcutta
where we won't touch.
We clutch what we own to our centers.
The homeless reside on their fingers
next to cement.

Dark Train Pulling

You, I haven't seen since the turn of the century.
There was a train then, always about to depart.
Or a letter traveling across Europe by rail.
A boat full of people who all looked forward
towards a better life of tailor shops and diamonds,
away from the small villages of Estonia.

In the old country, you lived in Hungary
but you weren't Hungarian. Russia,
but you weren't Russian. You were only a Jew
and not allowed to purchase land.
I want you like my people wanted soil.
That was the trick, my wanting and your no.

Denial works to wed a past to longing.
And now, like a promised land, you arrive.
Startling horizon, your suitcase,
something foreign stamped on the side.
A message I've needed all my life,
"Lose everything," it says, "You know how."

You arrived from the other country,
the past, dark train pulling, sparks over coal.
At death, there's another tunnel.
Of all the faces and the bright light,
yours will still beckon towards a bliss.
My dark hair, your dark hair, an America.

The Russian Room

I've spent the day among photos,
I'm that calm. All day
you aren't my husband
but I hear your music.
I saw the red embroidery
from Hungary hang on the wall
of our mutual friend.

Now I ride the peaceful train south,
Mt. Kisco, Chappaqua, Valhalla.
I'm so tired, I want your shoulder.
The man across the aisle
studies osmosis, that lucky voyage,
while I feel New York on me like a suntan.

I was playing Risk-all,
that open-mouthed game adults try.
A Russian roulette without bullets,
just you and me in the Russian Room
full of water glasses and napkins.

Adultery is a word with perfect pitch,
has inside it sultry and the necessary pain.
The heart, I hear, has more room than blood.
After a lover, there's a wet scent
that I never fail to know.

It's Grand Central, time to gather
up my things. Outside it rains.

I hail a taxi, ride it right through
my money like I'm sane. I call you up
while my clothes are still wet.

There's not much to say.
I run my finger around a wine glass
to make her sing. I take my place
in the album beside you, want to be
in black and white on the last page.

Brevity

The great and frightening thing
about being adults
is that by now we know
we can't save each other.

I came to you out of long-term marriage,
institutionalized, but great benefits and views.
And you from solitude, that study you've made,
New York libraries, jazz festivals, the road.

Over sushi we were delicate, gave our best,
told stories of men and women
in condensed detail, more entertaining
than anything on Broadway.

The next night, this time Italian,
I almost strangled on arugula,
laughing and leaning against the wall
at our ridiculous and certain lives apart.

Then I cried, drunk on very little wine.
I offered money for your body, all my cash.
I quoted Zorba the Greek on women's invitations to bed,
watched the waitress who knew you well watch me.

We got out of there, walked toward mid-town.
The marquee as we kissed goodbye
lit the already lit 87th and Broadway.
"Women on the Edge of a Nervous Breakdown" showing.

And you, with your immaculate kind hand,
left me there to my own beauty,
that place you took me sightseeing.
A brief holiday. Then you back
to your music and notebooks, me,
into the rough and verdant garden of family love.

Bardo Blues

for D.G.

"Your body is so quiet in heaven"
    LINDA GREGG

Fifty-three days into your death, the bardo
a holiday you look back on. It is so silent
without your gravity, the music of your fingers
on another woman. I eat and ache, solid Eros.
I was never maternal in your presence.

Your body is reduced forever, the weight
you fought off has fallen onto others.
Sorrow is a barge or a rafter, or an article
about war or an article of used clothing.
A sweater, for example, after a plane disaster.

Of all the sorrows, I felt yours less
than anyone's. Your temperament is glass
and mine is wood. Your soul was woolen
and mine an armoire. You took a wife
and I already was a wife.

It is so quiet in heaven and on earth
as if God continues making silence
despite all we've ruined.

Jazz at the Blue Note

On Broadway we said maybe when we're sixty,
then you got married and that was one thing.
Then you died young. That was another.
And I am still married, the third. But here
I am on the day after Christmas, sitting
around with friends and my sweet husband
is telling the same story, medicine wheel,
brujas, quantum physics, the works and you
come to me and I think, oh shit, I'm sixty-two
and you're gone and there are old loves
out there and then there's my weight and
white hair. What are these lost loves for?
There's no second chance, just this sixty seconds.
I think of Broadway that night, and the clock
you threw against the wall and the black long-
sleeved tee shirt and elevators that only rise.

Triolet à Trois

I'm cleaning house for Victor HernándezCruz.
Don't ask me why, he's not even my type,
back in Puerto Rico with his white suit.
I sing, cleaning house for Victor Hernández Cruz,
a man who drinks with his hands the world's blues.
Some male poets fill my ears with hype,
but I'm cleaning house for Victor Hernández Cruz.
Don't ask why. Invent it as I type.

Sometimes to clean you have to have a lover,
a man walking out the screen door into lilac,
down into the garden, through the arbor
in a white suit. Any man cleans into a lover.
He says, your husband's onto you, you're clever.
Beyond romance, I'm known in common fact.
Sometimes you clean your old house, take a lover,
fill vases with dreamtime or a man outdoors in lilacs.

Flowers are swollen, the night's a balm.
Nobody home, my music soft, the polyphonic bullfrog night
reminds me of Puerto Rico, or New York, Jazz clubs. Calm
as flowers swollen, the night's a balm.
The man removes his white suit from my arms.
Marriage is anti-aphrodisiacal, it causes flight.
The flowers are swollen; no night's a balm.
Everybody home, music blasting, the bullfrog night.

Solid as Chocolate

"I want to do with you
what spring does with the cherry trees."
    PABLO NERUDA, *Twenty Love Poems*

We live together, the thing is
I'm always right. You're always right.
Quirks. You knew it. You came to me,
tiptoed over the sea of poems

on my Chicago basement apartment floor
to my bed on the floor, loved me
in full sight of the typewriter,
its silent keys already taking notes.

And I use you in poems, and you use me
in jokes. And in bed, in bed, we use
each other, we use each other up,
more rainfalls in our hearts.

And where is your new heart?
Out in the oat fields, out in the barn
milking with your father. Up in the mountains
fishing for the one white trout.

Today I was driving into town, crying. I love you
more than an enemy. I need you more
than city of Chicago needs Lake Michigan.
Don't ever die. Don't ever run off

with whatever other woman loves you more.
She'll be just as impossible as I am
once you get to know her. Valentine.
You prefer horses, Brahma bulls, a fall.

"They're really solid," my friend the therapist
says. Sold as chocolate that melts,
is bad for your skin, expensive,
exploits workers in Mexico.

You're always right. I'm also right.
We live at right angles in a house
of right angles. You built the house,
the love is still under construction.

It can be hot one taken-for-granted day,
and the next, all the blossoms of Velarde,
New Mexico, the expanse of apples, the orchard
of apricots, all of us, freeze. I say this:
Consider the blossom and the fruit and the way
we fight towards love.

Heron Lake

You chose me and I chose you
a lake as blue as confidence.
Along the shore, what rock there is
is fragments. I stand
on crumbled sandstone.

The more distance, the more fragments.
There is no one truth.
There's the truth my body tells.
It won't lie to you, listen
at the place behind my knees.
That is my weather and the thick length
of me shows, middle age and all,
what's become of me.

I'm standing here alone
on the shore of Heron Lake.
It rains. My children
in a turquoise rowboat
with you at the oars. I'm slipping
away from family to solo admissions.
My lifetime laps out from this spot.

You are in a rowboat
going back and forth
for sheer momentum in this sleepy weekend.
In this economy, arm and water
equal movement. I long for another mind,
Wallace Stevens at Key West.

I have instead the oar's familiar sound,
The same plop and rip in all lakes
of the world. You have a square chin,
solid as the state of Wisconsin.
Even when unhappy with myself
I locate a place in you
where the boat returns,
a lake in the mountains.

Each other, each other,
the oars say.

Dark Fiesta

Fiesta floats go by on a night highway,
a festive décor of cornstalks and skeletons,
wildflowers and beauties waving.

There's danger in these mountains.
An avalanche buries,
I shovel you out of yourself.

You pinch my nipples. I bite hard.
Driving on black ice,
about to skid, getting from far to near.

I want to unbutton the 300 buttons
that run down the front of your soul.
Strip off the shirt you hide from me in.

Climb down into the basement
so we can make more noise. Sure,
go to the bathroom first. Start empty.

Cats assemble outside our door,
scratch all the way to bare wall.
Your ground is my sky.

Rescue, rescue, it's only one patent cure
that works well for a while
for absolutely everything obdurate and cold.

Talk to me. Open the slit your face that lipstick
covers. Fling me from myself, my hometown.
Rape my name by saying it too loud.

Change me. Polish my toenails red.
Show me the inside of the out,
the dark faces of love, all the dark harvest.

The Sugar Orchids

Sometimes in the night he is a beautiful
and mysterious husband. He brings me to orchids.
He ingratiates my thighs with kisses
he never had for any other wife. He takes the knife
out of the day like King Arthur. He's impaled
on the rock of marriage, rescuing each dollar,

fixing each alarm.
His fingers play "Au Claire de Lune."
I'm strummed. He borrows the night for me
from old women in black dresses.
His tongue is not afraid, he licks
the sugar skulls from Mexico.

He invited the clematis to grow up the bedstead
because they need their roots in the dark.
Contradictory vine, their blossoms need sunlight.
If I'd lie I'd say, their fragrance is grape,
but I'm truthful. They only flower
in sex, as everything tonight is wearing mystery.

Clematis is married to the trellis, morning
glory to strings up the eastern window,
flagrant blue, opens shameless in daylight.
Daylight astounds me, just how classical daylight
is, a formal arrangement of pain and duty.

I want to live at night now. Send the children
to school, position the shutters for noon
to go black. Send the parcel post man
to deliver me from daylight. Night blooming cereus
is so rare, the women wait up weeks
until is blooms. I'm like that now. I'll poise
here for flowering.

And old women in black dresses pin on a corsage.
They say, "Be young. Be brave and young for us."
I wear their sorrow and their flowers.
Nobody could get any younger,
you couldn't get the sugar orchids any sweeter.

I Don't Know Wide But I Know Deep

We mated with skin that could be from any century.
There is no tattoo on the body
of the man I love. There is no work
too long or too hard for the man I love,
including me with my curious ardor for pain.
He can take dark like anything on earth.

I want to love him till we're bruised.
My arms with a mark of wings,
Tantric art on my shoulder, a symbol
the shape of his teeth.

If he had breasts he'd be my perfect lover,
some extra softness where the heart sounds.
I'm his Parisian, he's my American.
The war could begin any minute. It's urgent.
Let's decorate the instant with sin.

There is no memory in the belly of the man I love.
My head rests there, has rested, will rest,
a conjugation of peace. There is no money
in the pocket of the man I love.
We can have everything, Paris in the thirties,
small cafés, women dance with women,
men with men, all dressed to kill.

He's naked. He's wearing black,
I'm all in cotton and silks.

Under that part that puts on garments,
deeper than the place which circulates blood,
grows the great spacious face
of the love I love, an arrival
more pressing than winter.

Torch singers, contortionists,
all of us came from this,
sacred assembly of skin.
Shot full of stars, I enter him.
Something larger and larger
takes up the room. Open
the windows, he calls.
Open them.

Hindu

The husband finds the wife more lovely
than she finds herself. And she sees him
younger than the world. Is this not love?
The other morning her legs framed his face,
a sacred text of sex between them. Too
Kama Sutra, they both came undone
with laughter.

        Outside the window
a perfect waning moon. Plowing her,
a farmer. Framing him, an artist.
In the other the beauty each had a heart
from lacking. Tarnish on silver is found
by some to give a luster more stirring
than polished sterling. She sang a raga
without knowing, in the tones
that issued forth out of her coming.

Post Coital

All day post coital, you reverberate
both man and woman. Even our therapist
says you look handsome. I'm name you
Mr. Tzedakah, which means of good quality.

I'm storing up for winter. There's
always another winter and an Egypt.
tear out the raspberries, the pyracantha,
the goat heads, the locust, the rose,

anything with thorns. Last night, half
a white moon planted asters, half
a dark moon sobbed. I came from coal dust.
You came from milk. We met in wind from the lake.

Even Kabala has a place for your leg
a place for my leg, rungs of the same ladder,
branches of the same tree. We were flying up
all night and we were climbing down.

We held hours before action, it was less
Italian and more Viennese, that is to say
waltz and not tarantella. My mother met
your father and flirted.   Your mother baked

a pie for my father. All night was a washing
as if the leaves cleansed their hands with rain
before a meal. I only saw you once since morning.
You said my lipstick accentuates chamisa.

Your head is still on my breast. My hand
around you. Throb is a word more autumnal today.
Aspens throb as much as quake. Hearts cha cha.
Seasons migrate like geese or grown children.

If I weren't so happy I'd be forlorn,
like her eyes under the word *divorce*.
I'll go there with widows and divorcees
and men with AIDS avoiding Fire Island.

The Dalai Lama has never felt like this. I have
no system for this loving, except the four
seasons and the four chambers of the heart,
the four emotions: joy, fear, sadness, and pity.

Grace of last light on roadside wildflowers.
Graves at the Jewish cemetery need tending.
My own graven image on your chest, miraculous
shroud where my face stains your shirt.

Speaking of Happiness

I want you to be happy so I look to the rain.
Lotus grew on the lake
on the way to the Pure Land.
Maybe you'll never be content
this side of death. Paradise
is a walled garden. You don't believe
in walls, though a good fight
and a barbed-wire fence will do.
When rain falls through, no snags.

I watered all the plants
with rainwater, trying to soften
the life we've aged. I look at
what gravity taught you last fall
hunting elk at Santa Barbara, saint
of fire. Riding out alone with our horses
Blanco and Dollar Bill. Two.
And you. Gravity calling.
The rain and the elk calling
each other for love at night.

It is sweet to smell you back
from the hunt. The rain all night
though we were estranged
rang a perfect tone. Childhood
farm rain, city rain. Unborn
rain. Duty and commerce gone.
Time to milk cows for rain.

Time to harvest bread-and-butter
corn. Time to be happy this side
of the grave. Where gravity
told you all about love.

Qualicum

(place where the big fish pass)
Qualicum Beach, B.C., 1996

I gave him a flower
from Qualicum
and by the end of the hour
we had crushed it, crushed
it, we had torn all the purple
from the stalk.

I brought him the flower
with a name I hadn't learned,
I was only loaned its fragrance and shape
which was exactly his shape
in a certain slant and mood.

As on this morning, after
the sun rose inside my old chests
and "Las Mañanitas" played me back
to New Mexico. Tears for departure.
We'll linger here, let the ferry go
and catch a later one,
crossing to Horseshoe Bay.

I brought him an unnamed flower
so he loved me back to India
and the story of Ganesh, who moves
the unmovable across three continents,
through time zones and two thousand years

where temple walls are carved
with voluptuous embrace, and Shiva
and Shakti speak in whispered syllables.
There are other lifetimes at stake.

We, old lovers too, carve a fragile frieze
into momentary sheets. Our blessed limbs
and hearts will not be chronicled here.
Can only be sung in the days
before the Vedas were written down
by the elephant with four arms,
connoisseur of sweets, remover
of obstacles, who gave me a flower
from a tree on the boulevard

outside our rented room, highway thick
with truck sounds that we used
to hide our own sounds at the Sunset
Inn at Qualicum this morning.

After Our Silver Anniversary

Third night in our own bed.
Finally the rains flatter the new
red roof. You tap me like we tap
maple for its rising blood.

You find your sweet way home.
Lightning visits our room.
The bell of night rings.
Red rain soothes our red roof.

Vajra to meditate upon
during my first childbirth
and by my third I was looking out at clouds,
quoting Mirabai, "Without the energy

that moves mountains, how am I to live?"
In the middle of love my friend
who is dying lies down in my mind.
What we do is the prayer for him.

As we both let go, rebirth, miracle,
resurrection, all manner of impossible
acts in this simple bed where our child
was made and born. We grow terrible

with love, and the rain
after so much drought
smothers doubt, too. Thunder,
a pillow to muffle our noise.

We have heard God's voice only
in privacy. We make time. Then
a few words. What are words
when we live so briefly in bodies?

What are bodies but ground
for the birth of hearts?
We come home to love and make
sacred forms older than temples.

Gesticulations

If I grow older and lose all memory,
Having no more dates and only names that serve,
If you are beside me, I will put my hand
In your back pocket. Blue jeans never age.
My hand alive against you.

If I have no hands, I will place my heart
Under your hat. I will smell your hair
With my reliable heart, and love how colorless
Your hair smells. I can tell we haven't grown wise.
We'll fight our fabulous fights

Grown fuller and fuller of laughter. The same
Fights fought so long they'll be choreographed.
A stiff old Russian ballet with many leaps.
You will be kissing my Bolshoi hem and I
Will curtsy in the next millennium.

If I have no heart, I will bite into your arm.
I will follow by my teeth, leaving curved marks.
I'll taste how your arm has done so much for me,
Carried things in from the trunk, brought me to pleasure
And pain, built the house, swaddled the child.

If I'm toothless and vision gone,
If I am bodiless, if I'm dead before you,
I will still be a gesture in our daughter's shoulder.
She will shrug and it will be my indifference.
She'll smile, I'll be flashing semaphore.

This rehearsal of loss so I can feel the life
We actually are. Not the taxes we pay
On the love we've cashed, but anxious holy love
Driving over the washboard road. We've scrubbed
Each other clean, rubbed each other right and wrong.

It is finally sinking in, total recall,
These gestures of thick and thin, once and for all.

One Kind of Door

for Bill Gersh

There is a large 100 year old
bank vault on my chest.
You put it there when you decided
to die. Would you kindly remove
the bank vault door, manufactured
in Akron, Ohio, and replace it
with miraculously living. Stranger
things have happened on this earth.

Walking around with a slightly
floating door before my heart could impede
the progress of western civilization as seen
from my Pittsburgh eyes, into your Catskill
eyes. The 21st century might never come.
A siren outside at 4 AM in the dark country.
News of your illness fixes my mortality,
a pinned bumblebee to my forehead.

I write this with a Children's Hospital
Telethon ballpoint pen to prove
how sincere ink is. I tried to get
Allen Ginsberg to write this for you, but he
was celebrating his old beat age. I asked
Nazim Hikmet. He was admiring your art
with the perspective of Turkish death
which is as strong as Turkish coffee.

So I had to write it, humbly
and with love. Smelling all around the stunning
air of Lama Mountain, where lilacs make saints
appear and open trap doors.

What I've Noticed About Death

Is that after the breathing stops,
the world starts breathing us.
Odd objects recollect us and exhale.
I can't drive north because my compass
needle is Bill Gersh, last seen as ashes.

Lilacs have already told me
all about the past. Make a shrine
of Cadillacs and soap. Collect the toll
in Yiddish. Tears for breakfast.
Pancakes in the underground garage.

My dead insect collection starts
singing about cicadas and romance,
the puta bumblebee, the fast millipede
for the end of the millennium.
Not to mention superficial mosquitoes singing scat.

Say the word underpants once in your voice
and my husband's sobs flew into May
like airmail straight from grief. Par Avion.
Hasta baby. Your elegy is made of chrome
and oil paint. The color wheel, a map of France.

I recommend my art to study with your breath
learning the wild pleasure of truth. Poetry,
you'd say, is something absent when the light's on.
Schmear prayers on us dumb mortals.
Tell whatever God gobbled you to spit

your spirit out whole, tangy, breathing
that God breath. *Mazel* to your daughters,
old colossal, rain down mitzvahs, hold
the *tsuris*. Giving all our middle years
an alpine glow. Good sunsets from Lama Mountain,

old hubcaps and white jackets. In immortality,
I hear your voice now, healthier than last week,
nothing like zero for clean bill of health.
Perfecto once more. One Gorgeous Grief.
Bill Gersh, I'm tearing my clothes into Yiddish.

I want to sit *shivah* with a *minyon* of artists
and say the *Kaddish* all night, I'm not sleepy.
Cover the mirrors so they won't see us dancing.
You can drink anything in heaven and send me down
your holy drunkenness for my new enriched art.

Irish Poem for a Zen Wake

For Robert Winson- October 23, 1995

For he was a peach and I missed his death
like you hail a taxicab, and you'd gasp
at how it drove away and I missed the train
and the apple crashed, the apple fell too soon.

He was the freshest one I knew
in a world rotten with greed.
From the velvet of first meeting him
to the last lines that we spoke.

He was the one nobody spoke ill,
and he was the one with disease.
And he was the kindest man to me
for putting me at ease.

Even on the bed of death he treated me
like a host. For he was a peach
as fresh as "to bless," he was kind
as the Florida sea at calm, glossy as that sea.

For he was the friend who married my friend
and they both have sung through me,
and the both have sung me higher
than I was able to hold.

And they gave me good and held me there
in the high plain of their regard.

They joked with me and they took my words
and planted them on their farm.

He was my friend. He asked me to leave
so he could find some sleep. But he didn't forget
in his final days to allow that life was deep.
He told me love and I put my lips

on the side of his emptiness.

I walked out from the hospital
with a hole as salt as the sea.
And I took a bite of that life of his
and hungry ghosts all around.

I went on the road to do the gig
and he died in that sprawling town.
I wanted to sing him into the end.
There's plenty time now to sing.

I wanted to be a prayer that rose
at the side of my darkling friend. We never have
enough to give, or so it seems to me.
I knew I had nothing to bring to him

so I brought him my emptiness.

The hour I sat felt like too short
but my watch told me it was too long.
He asked me to leave with delicate grace
and he asked me to leave with my emptiness.

I flew north to perfect my song. For he
was a peach and he was a gem, wait till you see
how wide, the community and the wild array
of people at his side.

The wide array of how much he knew and the sweetness
of his time. We are how wide his heart has been
in the emptiness, in the sweet life juice,
in the prime in the prime in the prime.

Ash Sutra

No more body
light years turning the hair
white, then flame.

My friend is a widow now
dust on her shoes, dust
of the plain song, dust of the
underworld, dust of the cracked egg,
dust of the mercantile, dust
from the Beatnik road, dust made of
powdered light, dust of the
morning bread, dust of the fashion
show, my friend is a widow with
light on her window sill, light
on her picture frames, light in
her every tear, light on the radio.
My friend is a widow
with fire all around him now
Zen monks are chanting
the Prajna Paramita
smoke filling Santa Fe, my
friend is ashes now, ash on
a Pittsburgh street, ash on
the cigarette, ash in suburbia,
ash on the radio, ash from the Ashcan
School, ash from Bar Mitzvah boys,
ash in the heroin, ash on the aspen
leaves, my friend is a widow now
carrying her husband. My friend
is a widow now with dust on her shoes.

Grief's Entitlement

I want to be perfect for your grief
mourn sixty times less than you do
for you are the widow. As God gave
us honey as a sixtieth of prophecy
sleep as one sixtieth of death.

I want to be perfect for your grief,
don't want to take anything.
I stole all your husband's pens
so I could write this. I sorted
his paperwork, so I could relinquish him.
Letter after letter asking, Are you alive?

Each time I see you I say one off, stupid thing.
My mind cranks out errors, we're flawed
we're flaw, we're flawing. I want
to be at your side or on your telephone.
I want to be kinder and funnier, first
thing I want is to be perfect for your grief.

I want to be just the right amount sadness
and the right amount lightness, but the
formula's eluding me. I want to be human
for your grief and that includes error.
We're flawed were flaw we're flawing
the temple bells perfectly ring.

Ode to Grief

My mother took the blond out of the world.
My grandson returned it, leaving the blond
intact. But grief has a life not its own
dwelling in the carrier, an infection
not fatal, causing no fear, hidden germ.

A drawer of hankies, the solace of soft folds.
Some days you take them all out and iron.
Your mother returns, her perfume lifts
from the steam. Straighten out all
the monograms, they stand for beauty.

I kept one black sweater, acrylic with silly
embroidered bees buzzing an artificial hive.
Queen Bee, it says, and I keep it there
next to my father's blue pajama top,
actually a drawer apart but I'll reunite

for grief will have its weird ways with us.
You run the washing machine with no clothes.
You keep a mink stole in you closet till
you die. You have a file marked DEATH.
I plan a book of my dead, insertable pages

as the dead only add as they subtract.
Grief is a page then, something I can
manage, not a football field of hair
or a manicure by God. The cheeks hollow.
Grief happens underneath age.

Our finest friend flirts one last time.
My cat is put down with the same heart
my mother lingered with. Wring out
the sponge of tears. Don't medicate
or grief will burrow in.

Worm ridden wood, moths in the mink,
the cashmere scarf eaten, all grief's
handmaidens bringing small loss. Praise
grief. People ask if I've lost weight.
I've lost the weight of a mother, a cat,
a red-headed friend in the Rio Grande.

Come Ons

"I have stumbled lost and wild onto sacred ground,
Now I'm frightened like a child in my last go round."
ROSALIE SORRELS

Everyday I get junk mail for life insurance.
Someday I am going to die.
My daughter sleeps upstairs in a pink Sphinx tee-shirt.
She can't stop me with her clenched love.

The sunflowers' faces bow, the lettuce bolts,
the beets grow woody, and my freezer
a chest full of last year's chile, old apricots
and one flicker frozen solid that still shocks me.

Large breasted women walked down the streets
before me and after me. And someday, I am going to die.
Yesterday was another birthday. They come and go.
Large breasted women hug me to their chests,

offer me birthday cake. Someday I am going
to die, birthday cake or no, exactly and at great
distance. The first year we planted pine trees
north of the house. The trees all grew, made windbreak.

A shelter of our hands even in absence. The pine trees
we planted all died and the wind knocks the north window.
We never planted. They never grew. It became intention
with its earning power of zero. Someday I am going

to die. I clear my desk of mail describing term-life,
my investments are my time, my life now, that large lion
sings and roars. Today I am going to write first,
later there's time for other considerations.

AUGUST 24, 1989

The Highlight of my Day

At the dump with my darling
reading Jack Gilbert and Linda Gregg
who dedicate their books to each other.
I dedicate this trip to the landfill
to you, who said, "Life is full" this morning.
My commentary on the recyclables
is not always appreciated. But
we love each other plentifully
in plenty America, at the dump
with two dragonflies, double helicopters,
copulating midair.

MIRIAM SAGAN

Invocation: The Art of Love

New moon, darkness, a white
Chrysanthemum
In an antique silver vase
Not belonging to your grandmother
But gift of a sometime lover.
Miriam, you say, why don't you
Tell the truth for once
All those stories about love
You save up like spare change
In a jam jar
Men and women, women and women, men with men
Everything you've ever done
Or heard about
Or wanted to do again
And please, you say, don't start
Learning ancient Greek
In preparation
Or translating awkwardly from the Latin
You know it all—
Bad-boy Cupid on his motorcycle,
Weapons and border skirmishes,
A hard bed,
Someone asking for money,
An abortion, and
The throb of Isis Isis Isis
Just before the room shifts red.
There is no remedy for love
Even the poet who should know

Simply said: Love is a kind of war
And no assignment for cowards.

The Princess and Curdie
after George MacDonald

Safe in bed on the floor
In a valley of the city,
You read the fairy book aloud:
"A mountain is a strange and awful thing,
Heart of the earth escaped
From the dungeon, heart not of blood but
Buried sunlight that keeps the earth alive."
I put my lips to your ear, kiss:
When the door is opened
Floor falls away, beneath our feet
An abyss, starless,
And a moon shining inside the room
Spinning like an enormous wheel.
After love, we return and sit naked.
You take my photograph,
Hand me a cup of chocolate, and tell
My fortune with cards and stars.
"Shapes are only dresses,
And dresses are only names."
The room smells faintly of burning roses.
At breakfast we tell the dream of earthquakes
Recurring throughout this neighborhood.
A crystal breaks light, scatters rainbows.
The book ends: "One day at noon
The whole city fell with a roaring crash,
Cries of men, shrieks of women,
Then a great silence."

We kiss good-bye and I walk out
Into the street. I want
To gaze into an emerald, magic,
To see if you are safe.

The Animal Husband

For a long time, unmarried, I
Kept to clean sheets, my own blood,
Kept to daylight, where men remain men,
Slept alone.

Then you arrived with berries and cream,
Wooing with mushrooms, roots in a human form,
And I married you
Dark beard and chest of fur.

And you became a badger
Clever, sleepy, fierce,
The earth your house
We burrow deep.

By air you are raven,
The wise thief,
Stealing a bright ring
Or a piece of meat.

I remain a woman, so I think
But you call me raccoon
Washing in the stream
Giving you a bite and a kiss.

Valentine

We lived together on Rose Alley
In a slum under the freeway
It was a good place to get married
Or to lean out of the window and yell "police."
Now I want to send you a sailor's valentine
Be Mine, shark spine
Think of Me, cowrie
Make a Wish, starfish
Not Uncertain, sea urchin.
I want to embroider you a sampler
I love you ABC
I love you XYZ
L-O-V-E
In chocolate from TG & Y
Because I'm sorry I tore your favorite green sweater
Yesterday afternoon in the Taos municipal parking lot
But you know the reason
Now I want to send you a pair of cut-out hearts
Doily white like grandma's antimacassars
Or a pair of black tombstones
Two green cypress trees grown together.

Love Song

Crossing the river gorge
Deep into mountains

Two bodies into one
Make a cipher, hexagram

I love you as much as mesa, New Mexico
Covered in sunflowers, covered in roses

Covered in peach trees
Covered in volcanoes

Tamarisks in the middle of the afternoon
We make a word of flesh

And with the sheets falling off
And the shutters drawn

Against the brilliance of our skin
That ideogram

The Sailor

Jason and the argonauts in full-blown color
Poised in snapshot
Lifting the golden fleece
Or leaning like low riders
On old Chevys, pink fuzzy dice
Over the dash. The utter stupidity
Of heroes—
Their boats with two Egyptian eyes
Painted on the prow
Have more sense than they do
To go with the wind.
Every man looks at his fate and starts running
Away from it, back into its arms
Jason loves Medea
The little hairs on his brawny arm
Don't stand up in terror at her name
He isn't halfway through
She's just a girl
She likes him
She'll do anything for love.

Once, long ago, there were two lovers
Also a golden fish and a Moslem moon
Magician in a trance
Can speak to the dead husband
Who has married again in the land of the dead
And is building a new house there.
Personally, I wish you liked me better

And didn't care so much
About getting your own way.

The Russian poet in prison
Knows her husband will wait
Out her sentence alone in the apartment.
In solitary she reads her poem along the empty pipe
To common criminals, hookers and burglars
In their separate cells.
And the tap tap comes back with a question
"Who is this guy Ulysses?"
That is what I want to know myself
Which one of us is on an island
With Calypso, that low-tide lady
Which one of us keeps house
In the expensive palace eternally in need of repair.
Who sails from the past, blasted like an ancient column
Who waits, who waits
Who weaves the imperfect picture
Of a dissolving reunion.

He Dreams

Alive, he dreams of Key West
Alley behind the Cuban bakery
Strip of palms screening a shack
A good feeling of anticipation
Like turning over a rock and finding a turtle.
Alive, he dreams of a basement
Full of tanks of fish
He has neglected to feed
The tanks are overgrown
Fish shine like neon
In the window of a cocktail lounge.

Dead, he dreams of me
He dreams I am standing in the kitchen
In a white nightgown he has never seen
I am holding a vegetable cleaver
That has been improperly sharpened
Attempting to cut a blood orange into quarters.
In the dream he wants to yell:
Use a different knife
Do you know how many people I've seen
Cut themselves that way?

Dead, he dreams about the proper equipment:
A bag for the binoculars,
The best snow shovel,
A good pen, an extension cord,
A tiny microphone, an electric bass.

Dead, I dream of him
Back in the house,
Angry that I've given everything away.
Alive, he dreamed his body
Was being cut up and thrown into the sea.
Alive, he dreamed of Key West
Of an ocean
Where any flesh was bait for the unexpected.

I Know Who You Are

Last night I dreamed that you weren't dead
We'd broken up
You were still sick, but well enough
To hold a job
I yelled at you on the phone: why the hell
Can't you come home once in a while
And read your daughter a good night story?

You are a 36-year-old ghost—
You will never be any older
In the photograph your head is shaved, zen priest
You wear a red T-shirt, you smile
You hold a doll's head
Which you are repairing
You haven't looked this good in years.

You are my first husband.
You are my husband
You are a four-month-old dead person
Like a four-month-old fetus
No one can feel you move
I might still abort or miscarry you,
Like a developing baby
With each month you become increasingly
Dead.

Now you are a reason--
The reason acquaintances embrace me

My friends enquire of each other: how is she?
The reason a man who is not you
Tells me on the phone: I love you
Passionately
You are the reason I won't listen
To Otis Redding
The reason N. has a flashback, A. hates her husband,
L. weeps, that my phone bill is $500.

I know who you were:
Near-sighted, hilarious,
Bad-tempered, a terrible driver,
The only person I'll ever know
Who read Shakespeare in a dull moment for pleasure
I know who you are: ash, bone,
A name, my tears,
Mail that arrives
That cannot be properly delivered
Nor properly returned

Handwriting

I see rain fall on the end of summer
Yellow chamisa and the orange leaves
Of my neighbor Grace's apricot tree.
I see rain smear color like memory,
Color draining out of the world
Like New York City rainbow oilslick
Vanishing down the sewer grate.

Your handwriting is still everywhere in my house
You had beautiful handwriting, clear and bold,
And it has outlasted you.
I keep the bits and pieces
I couldn't bear to throw away,
Your calendar where the last thing written
Is "surgery"
And then the rest is blank.
The mail arrives for me, for my child,
For you, for the couple who lived here,
For Angel who doesn't live here,
Mail arrives for the dead and living.
I should take your name off the gas bill,
I should take your name off the electric bill.

I read your notebooks without fear of revelation.
After all, years ago,
You burned those love letters from Miss X
In a tin can in the front yard of the old apartment.
I don't see your ghost on the corner

The way your friends and sisters can
To be honest, I don't want you around
You're dead, I'm not, we have to break up
As surely as if you'd run off to Cleveland with Miss X.

I believe I will be happy.
I am the only widow in my family
But I am not the most unhappy person.
I believe I will paint the bedroom pink
I will go to Hawaii, and to Trinidad, Colorado
I will buy red velvet to wear all winter.
Since you died I have danced at a wedding,
Been on three boats, seen falling stars
And been given a free papaya at the market.
I believe I will live to be old without you.

I see your handwriting
On the words of the Buddhist gatha
On the note saying: Mir,
Let's Have A Date.
I see your coat in the closet
I see your eyelashes on your daughter
Your smile in her smile
I see her sob, and hit the pillow,
Wailing for you.
I'm glad I don't see you as a ghost,
Thank you for not coming back.
The last time I saw you in a dream
You were lying in the bathtub
With your abdomen patched in black rubber.

You said: "Tomorrow I'll be dead."
I'd like to see you well in a dream.
I see rain falling over New Mexico.
I say: good-bye, I'll see you later.

Jack and The Beanstalk

The boy hangs upsidedown from the beanstalk—
You don't trust me, but you have no choice
I lie in bed listening to your voice
Come across invisible wires.
After midnight, I go out and plant
Some dangerous seed in hard winter earth:
A green pistachio nut, a dry kidney bean
A piece of my dead husband's bone in ash.
All night a vine will grow
Up to the giant's castle where things
Are much bigger than we are.

Last night I woke at 4 AM
Realized I had fallen in love with you
Again, irrevocably
I had locked you away
A heart that was still beating
In a box of gold with a silver key.
Now the box was open
I could hear it beating
As I set out to climb the beanstalk.

It is Valentine's Day, and hearts are everywhere—
You send me a chocolate heart
In a clear plastic box
But my daughter steals it and eats it.
My friends approve of you
But none of them knows

How hard it is
To climb this beanstalk
Which keeps rising into thin air.

I put a robe on over my nightgown
And put on my magic boots
I climb like a rock climber
On the face of Yosemite's El Capitan
I climb like my dead husband
Who once fell asleep in a sycamore tree
I climb like Jack
Whose mother knows he is a fool.
It is easy to find your heart
I slam the lid shut, grab the box, and run.
You don't trust me
Because 23 years ago I forgot
All about your heart.
I come down the beanstalk slowly
Like a toddler down porch steps
Like a yogi entering an asana.
I leave this great weed to stand
In my backyard—
A ladder for angels,
Staircase between heaven and hell,
Shaman's pole,
Like some dreadful Chinese elm
Whose roots will ruin
Thousands of dollars worth of plumbing.
I am ready to return your heart to you.
Or to keep it in my top bureau drawer

With the broken china doll, the condoms,
And my dead husband's sunglasses.
I am almost sorry
You know so much about me
For it will not surprise you that
You have my heart.

Andromeda's Tears

Star birth—star death
Rings of Saturn—Jupiter's moons
Or Pluto seen as a double planet
You and I circling each other this entire lifetime.
I am a woman with two husbands
One dead, one living
Widow, wife, or a girl
Chained to a rock
Waiting for the dragon.
Certainly you must be the hero Perseus
Who makes a living looking at things indirectly
Skinny and dark-haired, with a narrow face
Your secret is you don't care
About Medusa, that messy lady
With snakes for hair
Your secret is that you love me
Your secret is...
You didn't even know you had a secret.

My mother is a starry W in the sky
Cassiopeia, Queen of Ethiopia.
My secret is that as a child
I loved to pull leaves off bushes
Or shred the white strands of flowers
Called Andromeda's tears
And throw the hard blossoms across the yard
My secret is: I am not really
Chained to the rock
I am free to walk away at any moment.

I want to see what you can do to free me
You have a sword, and something dreadful in that bag
I want to see just how far I can travel
On the the kiss of a living man and ten thousand of a dead man.
Blue stars are born in clusters
A galaxy through the telescope
Might be a one-celled creature in a drop of pond water
My tears are free of everything but grief
What infects me is not contagious
I'm standing in the sky on this rock of stars
You can have me. Put out your hand.

More Than One Buddha

Yesterday, on Canyon Road
I took a turn into a courtyard
The gallery that had been there was gone
More than one Buddha adorned the lawn
Ten or twenty, thirty maybe
Cast from the same mold
Classic cross-legged, eyes cast down
Offerings in the lap of every one
Chrysanthemums, or asters, Mexican sunflowers
Attested that autumn was coming
Strings of prayer flags
Swayed above the garden
The cafe was closed.
Those Buddhas grouped in family arrangements
Remind me, husband, that you are dead
And gone off somewhere without us
Still, all day long
It pleases me to remember
What pleased you—
Umbrellas, teacups, shoes, rain.

Digging for Troy

A ruined city—
An image of the mind—
Layer upon layer—
Mound of grass that covers Troy,
City upon city, stratified in soil,
Laid down by history's alluvial flow
That you must sort
To find a story
Dig you must
Though victim and hero are both reduced to dust

My father read aloud from Lattimore's
Translations—*The Iliad, The Odyssey*
Unillustrated, line after line of Homer
Passed as a vision in my childhood brain
He'd pause sometimes, to wipe his eyes
Or blow his nose if truly overcome
He read both summer and winter
Before the fireplace, on the shady porch
I'd perch on the arm of the copious chair
Or sit across from him and watch him read,
It was obvious
Who his favorite was
Not a killer like Achilles
But the sailor Odysseus.

Helen is snatched, or splits,
That lovely girl

The beauty queen, homecoming royalty
Waving from the back of a float
All Helens have the same redundant fate
Beautiful, then old, their story
The narrative of who wanted them, for what.
She does not speak, a painted bride
Noh mask, her hand might gesture—
If she went for lust, or against her will,
No one will ask her.

The archeologist is on a spree,
Looking for his true version in the dirt
He cuts straight down into the story
Discarding other versions of the past
Digging through time
Falsely linear at this site
Like those gigantic redwood rings
I loved in childhood for their maps;
An arrow points: Columbus
Discovers America
As if this were a point of fact
For the growing tree.
After Troy, the archeologist slices down
Mycenea, where things too terrible
To speak of casually happened—
A husband murdered in his bath
A wife killed by her children
Adultery, murder, a girl
Who can't stop talking.
He digs down, his spade

Stopped by what he knew—just knew-—must be there
Kings' faces beneath golden masks—
His own face.

A lion gate, a beehive tomb
A golden goblet, silver moon
Carved crescent in the darkening sky
The student's head bent by the light of the lamp
Girl child with an abacus, parsing out arithmetic
Subtraction, loss, a numbered narrative
At the kitchen table.
An image tells you—what?—you've dug too far
Down beneath some heroic age
This pottery fragment tells you—what?
That what is broken cannot be replaced.

Every story has its start—
My sister once asked me
If I'd choose
To marry you again
Knowing in advanced how ill you'd fall
How you'd die young
Leave me behind, and with a grieving child.
Foresight is nothing,
Premonition's sense—a tingling
Of the hair along the arm
My whole life I was waiting
For something to strike
Coiled like a snake at the base of the spine.

After all, what about that reccurring dream
Of the sea, of the unstable house
Built without foundation
That lies simply on cinder blocks
As winter tide rises to engulf it.
After all, the fact is—you're still dead
Have left behind artifacts
Less enduring than Priam or Agamemnon
Kings at war, left a pair of rubber wader boots
A stack of unread mail,
Unpaid bills, a bicycle, a bicycle lock
Without a key.

The archeologist collapses in the street
Carried dying into the old hotel
His wife has worn the golden diadem
As Helen
Which will be stolen again
Snatched in the sack of Berlin
Gold taken to Moscow
Bronze to Petersburg
Nations collapse, reveal the horde
Of dangling wire, golden plume
A pendant lifted from a tomb
Blue glass, a woman's earring.

This jar is huge
What it contains
Oil, or wine,
Placental, will sustain

This jar might house a man.
This jar is huge,
It holds my grief
Contains what cannot
Be contained;
Peas and beans, sealed
And left behind
Stores of grain
Stashed behind a door of stone
These pithoi say—we will return
To cook and eat another day.
Instead, both queens and serving girls
Have disappeared, and gone away.

Troy's harbor now is silted
No ship can pass
The sea is barred
Salt memory of a past
That seeks you still.
Dry wind of quick-scented spring across the plain,
A green that's soon to fade,
On solid earth, you hold it in your hand
What light and shadow mottle,
If you could read, and understand-—
This message in a bottle.

Remarriage

My second husband says
He wishes my first husband
Would get married again—

My first husband
Has been dead for years,
But I dream about him.

At first, he was angry,
Or calling on the phone
Wanting to come home

But I was already
With the man who would become
My second husband.

Recently, I began to dream
My dead husband was dating
A very pretty—

But obviously not Jewish—
Blonde woman,
She seemed very nice.

My second husband
Was getting sick of my dreams—
He said he hoped they'd get married.

In my next dream
My first husband told me
He was indeed marrying her

But he enraged me
By inviting his sisters
But not our daughter to the wedding.

My friends politely mention
They think I am in denial
After all, my first husband

Is dead, not getting married.
But it is as if
He has some kind of life

That goes on without me
Perhaps because I have had
So much go on without him.

Mahler

Mahler's Ninth Symphony
Plays on the radio from the kitchen
You look up "romanticism"
In my dead husband's outdated Britannica.
One toe has worn its way
Through your frugal sock.

Night School

What I learned,
I learned in the dark—
Dreams of the sea
Beneath the house,
House on stilts
On the San Andreas fault,
Lit by neon
Pink and green
Like a sleazy bar
At the edge of nowhere.

What about that night
We came home early
Fell asleep, then woke again
Drank some tea, began to talk
Past midnight,
You lying on the rug
I on the bed,
We didn't touch,
Didn't need to kiss,
Needed instead
Words, poured out
Like dark wine from the bottom
Of the bottle

What I know
I know in the dark—
The shape of my feet,

The taste of my tongue,
My shadow in the mirror,
A blue bottle full of rosewater
Premonition, or deja-vu
Sleepwalker in a recurring dream.

Seabed

The sheets are full of sand
From your midnight swim

A body of water
Your body, which is water

Your kiss, which is a salt hex sign
Can ward off ill

Like a witch ball, glittering glass sphere
By the house on the harbor

Reflection to drive off spirits
Or bottle tree, each dead branch

Adorned with cobalt, amber, seagreen glass
Bottles to capture bad-intentioned ghosts

Divining for water
Watering with prayer

The sea has made its own bed
Let's go lie in it once more.

Round

You go out in the dark
Come back with hands full
Of stolen peaches—
Still fuzzy from the neighbor's
Old neglected tree
Fruit no one else will pick

Once in a deciduous wood
I saw a snapping turtle
Lay her eggs in the middle
Of a dirt road
After all our nights
Together under a half moon
I can't believe our luck
Won't hold again.

I Look At You

I really must love you—
It's obvious from the photograph
Of someone else's wedding
Where you and I sit
Leaning towards each other on folding chairs
You can't tell from the picture
But it has stopped raining long enough
For the well-apportioned bridegroom
And the pretty worried bride
To come down the aisle.

But we don't look
At them, we look
At each other, laughing
Romantically entwined, missing
The main action, forgotting to turn and look
At the tall groom and the short bride.

Something about this photograph
Might be French—the middle-aged couple
Ecstatic, the young bride
Squinting into the sun
That punctuates two rain showers
Which frame the ceremony beneath green cottonwoods.
What was I laughing about?
And now, embarassed to be caught
In the act, printed, then sent
On thank you notes to every guest,

This photograph.
We'd forgotten we were a subplot
In a larger story
Later, walking in moonlight
That fell over water
Beneath a wooden bridge
It was your face I searched it's true—
I looked at you.

Artichoke Heart

I cook this prickly thing for you,
Gently manipulate stiff leaves
Beneath cold water tap,
Rinse each hard green petal
Trim the stem, place it in the pot
Steam it. Like Eve
Holding a forbidden fruit
I set it on the table.
Did I stalk your heart?
An artichoke is rare, delicious,
Odd that one can both eat and choke on it.
You dip the pale green
Part of each leaf in butter,
I eat much faster than you do,
I eat more than my share,
"It's like lobster," you say
"I never know
What part I'm supposed to eat."
"Eat the heart," I say,
Artichoke heart on the stem
Steamy like a naked woman getting out of a bath.
I prune the prickles, slice that heart in half
Hand it to you.
"Saving the best for last?" I tease.
Later, I tell you, you know
You could buy two next time
I'd still cook them for you.
And you say: not until they're on special.

Did I mistake your thrift for love?
Did you really not just want to sit and dip
Those dark green leaves, that pale green heart
That thick stem?
Did you not want to look at me as you licked butter?
Middle-aged, you still have a green heart.
Young, you hitched through Castroville once,
The artichoke capital of the world
But you did not know how to eat an artichoke
Until you ate with me.

What I Know About You

1. THE THIRD PERSON

She crosses the avenue
Feet in Capezios, thin soles against hot asphalt
The man who sells
Slivers of roast lamb wrapped in pita
Sharpens his huge double set of knives
Winks at her
Crossing Broadway, waiting for the WALK sign to flash
In the heat she is sweaty
From hours of modern dance in a closed room
Being what—a sunflower, peace, a breeze
In her dusty leotard.
Walking east towards Chelsea
Uninspired brownstones
Not yet worth a great deal of money
A truck driver whistles
She gives him the finger
Buzzes at the apartment
He calls down: come on up, from the dormer window
He'll be naked in the heat
Cooking something—
What does he do
Until 4:30 PM when she arrives?
Her lover, not a boyfriend,
Though others would see a skinny nineteen year old
With hair that sticks straight up

With an addled expression of innocence
The kind of boy
One wouldn't fear
To pick up hitchhiking.
But she fears him a little
Hates him a bit as well
For despite the passion of his kiss
The meal he has cooked in the heat
He will never say the words:
I love you.

2. THE FIRST PERSON

I look in the mirror and ask you to zip my blue dress
The dress is both slinky and modest
So it satisfies both me and my mother
It is of some soft shiny material spangled with tiny white flowers
Thirty years later I will remember it
And you won't
I am seventeen and this dress
Looks like hundreds of dresses I will acquire
Throughout the course of my life.
You zip the back,
In the mirror, we look like a couple,
We are on our way to a Mostly Mozart concert
With tickets from my father
You will remember exactly what pieces were played
But not my dress.
I drape a strand of white beads around my neck
Feel both sophisticated and claustrophobic.

3. The Second Person

And now I see you coming towards me from a great distance
You shine with the blue and gold of a lost afternoon
The glamor of memory
As if I had always known you
As if you were my first love
As if your naked body in my bed resisted time
As if the sandpipers we saw on the sandbar
Who left tiny prints washed by the next wave
Were still alighting and flying off
As if the wind knew our middle names
The name that doesn't change, that is buried
In the parenthesis between given and family
As if it was your face in the mirror
Looking over my shoulder
Both young and old—you.

At the wedding
The guests argued about love
Versus lust
I looked at you in your hat,
Felt both.

have you ever
desired me
as much as I
desired you
in last night's dream?

When We Were Young

when we were young
we were meant
for each other

we were stupid
and went off hitchhiking
on other hearts

now that my hair is gray
I tell myself
I could barely live without you

for who else
wants to make love
like this

in a yellow room
off an overgrown courtyard
in a peeling bathhouse

at the little motel
in a hot springs town
at the edge of the Chihuahuan desert.

This Love I Use Daily

this love I use daily
like salt
like soap

the more I use it
the less there is
dissolved

the paradox
I don't miss it
but find it

everywhere, viejo,
your smile as you sleep
the blue door jamb

I find it in how
I don't live by the sea
but hear it in your left ear

how I've lived
beneath these mountains
for such a long time

The Yellow Bench

the yellow bench
in the sad garden
of spices

I see you pause
reading the book
marking the page with your finger

you've been dead
a long time
almost a dozen years

but here in the subtropics
you appear, as if in life
reading a book about birds

and smile the smile
that was yours alone to smile
ironic, a little wistful

as if surprised
by Fortune

yellow fruit has fallen to the ground
I was not here
to hear it make a sound of something overripe

and when I listen
for the rustle of the pages
of the turning book

you've gone away again
as I always
knew you would

Aubade

making love to you
in the single bed
in the forest
I drop an earring
black and silver beads
I bought from a Navajo woman
on the rim of Canyon de Chelly

that was a thousand miles from these firs and hemlocks
and a long time ago, too
but even then I was with you
though after a long absence

walking along the forest floor
you tell me how your time at the Pacific
reminded you of the desert
the same feeling—
maybe it was the horizon line
or the availability
of vastness

mushrooms—orange fairy caps and honey—
release their spores,
why, standing upright
is the future in front of us
the past behind?

my dreams have gills
can leap, amphibious,
although I'm never going back
to the place where I was born
but place
the unfamiliar cup
on the unfamiliar table
and move on.

There Is a Beach

sea pale green to navy to aqua
pink or pale beige sand

there you are
setting two plastic beach chairs
in the waves

there you are
carrying our daughter
on your shoulders

now you are gone

there is a beach

there are two figures
in the waves

they might be us
or in a snapshot from the fifties
someone's mother and father

now you are gone

it is 8 o'clock
I am reading a book
I am on page 14

it is 8:15
I am on page 36

I miss page 14
where the heroine
peeled an orange
in the dayroom

although page 36
is also pleasant
it has a train
and a sense of regret

the hands
of the clock move
and my hands
turn the pages
of the book
until the heroine
walks along the beach

the sea pale green to navy to aqua
the shore pebbly

you're gone

Two Small Paintings

two small paintings
of waves
sit in the nicho

I watch
the surf
suspended

white cap
blue green
changeable sky

in a place
meant for saints
I've placed water

and by extension
this bed's
a beach

and when we made love
this morning
I felt the sand on my back

Ten Little Death Poems

1.

I wanted to go
where I said
I would never go—
behind the rainy laurel hedge

2.

to be born
or to die—
either way,
you know
I'll complain

3.

in the run-down neighborhood
full of blown roses
I couldn't decide
how I felt
about this world

4.

waking after sleep
I'm often surprised
by my feet
on the wooden floorboards

you don't have to sleep
to be awakened
by the crow's guttural caw

5.
I was fifty
before I discovered
my opinion
barely mattered

6.
when the bell rings
the monk
puts on her flip-flops
shuffles down the corridor
to the meditation hall

7.
mother stumbles
towards the crying baby
the firefighter
reaches for a jacket
the cop for a cell phone
the EMT
promises herself
a cup of coffee
when this is over

8.
I realized that if the plane crashed
I wouldn't have to get off
and take care of anybody—
I began to relax in the cloud cover
over a coastal city

9.
and once you've had a taste
of dissolve
it is hard
not to long for more

10.
every country
has its exit visa

a bridgeless river
might just be a river

Biography & Acknowledgment

RENÉE GREGORIO

Renée Gregorio's poetry collections include *The Skins of Possible Lives* (1996), *The Storm That Tames Us* (1999), *Water Shed* (2004) and *Drenched* (2010). She's also published many chapbooks, most recently *Road to the Cloud's House: A Chiapas Journal* (2009, with John Brandi).

She has received grants for writing residencies at the Mabel Dodge Luhan house in Taos and the Millay Colony for the Arts in New York state. Since 1985, Renée has taught workshops in poetry and writing at the New Mexico Military Institute, the Taos Institute, the Harwood Art Center and Little River Poetics and was a visiting professor at Colorado College and a lead writer on a travel and writing course for San Juan College. In the past several years, she has conducted poetry dojos both locally and nationally.

Renée is a certified master somatic coach, writing coach and creator of the poetry dojo™, a learning environment in which participants engage in somatic and writing practices, exploring the wisdom of the body in relationship to the writing self, and removing obstacles to deep expression in writing. She holds a master's degree in creative writing from Antioch University, London, and a third-degree black belt rank in the martial art, aikido. She lives in El Rito, a small northern New Mexico village, with her husband, the poet and painter John Brandi.

"X at the Threshold," "X: The Space Between," and "The Final X" appeared in *The X Poems* (X Press, Santa Fe, NM, 1992).

"Circling Orgasmic" was published in an earlier version in the chapbook, *Circling Orgasmic* (12th Street Press, Providence, RI, 1992).

"Two" and "The Artist's Near-Wife: A Letter" appeared in the chapbook *When the Breathing Stops* (Yoo-Hoo Press, Farmington, NM, 1995).

"Measuring the Distance," "Bird-Death," "It's Raining in Augusta," "Letter to the Heart of My Far Country," "Partings," "Loose Change," "Valentine," "Rushes," and "Silent Dialogue" were all published in *The Skins of Possible Lives* (Blinking Yellow Books, Ranchos de Taos, NM, 1996).

"Your bare hand," "I hold strong coffee," "waking slowly," "This Harsh Desire for Other," "Triangle of Light," "God Went Away for the Winter,

She Said," "Bloom", "The Long Hill of Garrapata," "Reincarnate," "You, my husband, are", "The Painted and the Real," "The Storm That Tames Us," "The Beginning Island," and "Fragile Quartet" were published in *The Storm That Tames Us* (La Alameda Press, Albuquerque, NM, 1999).

"Indian Love Song" appeared in *Drenched* (Fish Drum Inc., New York, NY, 2010).

JOAN LOGGHE

Joan Logghe is Poet Laureate of Santa Fe 2010-2012. She works at poetry and arts activism in community, off the academic grid in La Puebla, New Mexico. She and her husband, Michael, raised three children and have three grandchildren. She studied at Tufts University where she graduated as Class Poet. Joan began a life in poetry by volunteering at her children's school thirty years ago and has worked with children and youth as well as adults, ever since.

Awards include a National Endowment for the Arts Fellowship, Witter Bynner Foundation for Poetry Grants, a Mabel Dodge Luhan Internship, and a Barbara Deming/Money for Women grant. Her teaching life has included Ghost Ranch Abiquiu, University of New Mexico-Los Alamos, Santa Fe Community College, Poets-in-the-Schools with New Mexico CultureNet, Artworks, Santa Fe Girls' School and Santa Clara Pueblo Day School. She taught poetry in Bratislava, Vienna, and Zagreb, Croatia in 2004.

Her books include *What Makes a Woman Beautiful, Twenty Years in Bed with the Same Man* (a finalist in Western States Book Award), *Sofia, Rice, and The Singing Bowl* from UNM Press.

"After Reading Love lyrics from India," "After Making Love," "Dark Train Pulling," "The Russian Room, "Brevity," and "The Homeless" appeared in a chapbook, *Poems from the Russian Room* (Superstition Press, 1989).

"A Lunch Date with Beauty" and "Reading in Bed," published in the chapbook *The Goddess Café/ A Lunch Date with Beauty* with Judyth Hill (Fish Drum #8, 1990).

"Dark Fiesta" and "Reading in Bed" appeared in the chapbook, *The Dark Faces of Love* (Yoo Hoo Press, 1992).

"Mixed Marriage," "Reading in Bed," "After Making Love," " After Reading Love Lyrics from India," "Pavilion," " The Homeless," "Dark Train Pulling," "The Russian Room," "Triolet a Trois," "Solid as Chocolate," "Heron Lake," "Post Coital," "Brevity," "I Don't Know Wide but I Know Deep," and "Dark Fiesta" appeared in *Twenty Years in Bed with the Same Man* (La Alameda Press, 1993).

"Speaking of Happiness," "Qualicum," "After Our Silver Anniversary," and "Gesticulations," appeared in *Blessed Resistance* (Mariposa Printing and Publishing 1999).

"Post Coital" was also published in *Seven Hundred Kisses: a Yellow Silk Book of Erotic Writing*, edited by Lily Pond (Harper San Francisco, 1997).

"Irish Poem for a Zen Wake," "Ash Sutra," and "Grief's Entitlement" were in a special issue of *Are We There Yet* dedicated to Robert Winson, 1995.

MIRIAM SAGAN

Miriam Sagan is the author of over twenty books, including the poetry collection *Map Of The Lost* (University of New Mexico Press). Her memoir *Searching For A Mustard Seed* (Quality Words in Print) won the best memoir award from the Independent Publishers Association in 2004.

Sagan founded and runs the creative writing program at Santa Fe Community College and advises the *Santa Fe Literary Review*. She has been a writer in residence in the Everglades National Park, Petrified Forest National Park, The Land/An Art Site in Mountainair, New Mexico, Stone Quarry Hill Art Park in upstate New York, and Andrews Experimental Forest in the Cascades.

She was married to Robert Winson, with whom she had a daughter, Isabel, until his death in 1995. Their joint diary *Dirty Laundry: 100 Days in A Zen Monastery* was published by La Alameda Press and re-issued by New World Library. She has received a grant from the Deming Foundation/Money for Women and won a Borders Library Association Award. In 2010, she received the Santa Fe Mayor's Award for Excellence in the Arts.

Sagan lives with her husband Richard Feldman on Santa Fe's west side.

"The Princess and Curdie" and "The Animal Husband," appeared in *Aegean Doorway* (Zephyr Press, 1984).

"Valentine" and "Love Song" appeared in *True Body* (Parallax Press, 1991).

"Invocation" and "The Sailor" appeared in *The Art of Love* (La Alameda Press, 1994).

"He Dreams," "I Know Who You Are," "Handwriting," "Jack and The Beanstalk," "Andromeda's Tears," and "More Than One Buddha" appeared in *The Widow's Coat* (Ahsahta Press, Boise State, 1999).

"Digging for Troy," "Mahler," "Night School," "Seabed," and "Round" in *Archeology of Desire* (Red Hen, 1999).

"Remarriage" and "I Look at You" in *Inadvertent Altar* (La Alameda Press, 2000).

"Artichoke Heart" in *Rag Trade* (La Alameda Press, 2004).

"What I Know About You" in *Map Of The Lost* (UNM, 2008).

"At the wedding" tanka and "Desire" tanka in *Tanka from the Edge* (Modern America Tanka Press, 2009).